Cracking the
SAT
Literature
Subject Test

2007–2008 Edition

Cracking the

SAT

Literature
Subject Test

2007–2008 Edition

Allison Amend

PrincetonReview.com

Random House, Inc. New York

The Princeton Review

The Princeton Review, Inc.
2315 Broadway
New York, NY 10024
E-mail: booksupport@review.com

Editor: Leanne Coupe
Production Editor: M. Tighe Wall
Production Coordinator: Ryan Tozzi

Printed in the United States of America on partially recycled paper.

9 8 7 6 5 4 3 2

2007–2008 Edition

Acknowledgments

I would like to thank the following people who assisted in the writing of this book: Suzanne Markert, Christine Parker, Lisa "Hawk Eyes" Liberati, Liz Buffa, and the New York City Public Library.

Thank you to Yung-Yee Wu and B. Young for their expertise in the art of writing diags.

A special thanks to Adam Robinson, who conceived of and perfected the Joe Bloggs approach to standardized tests and many of the other successful techniques used by The Princeton Review.

Contents

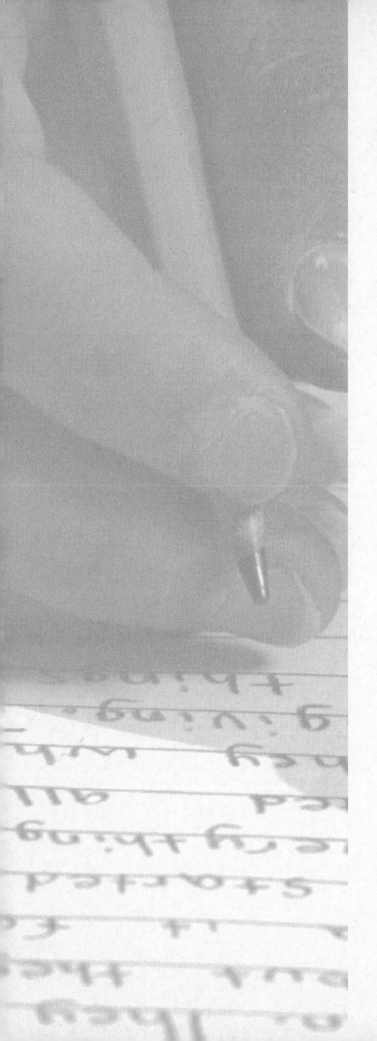

Part I
Overview

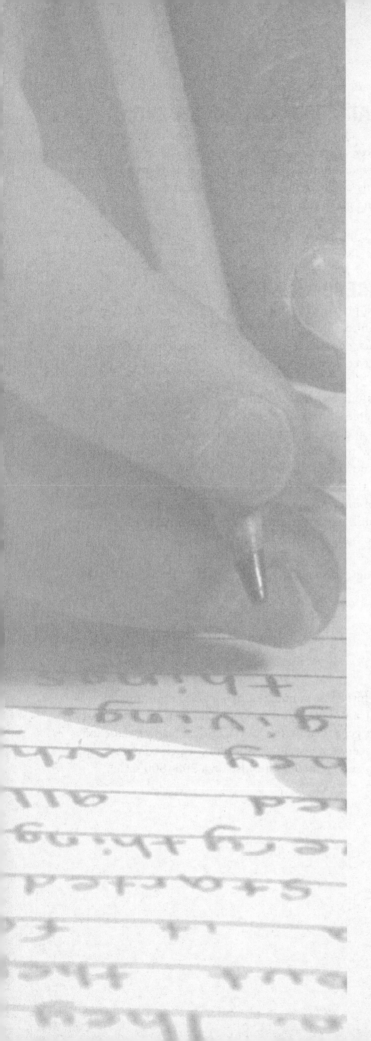

Chapter 1
The Route to
College

WHERE DO STANDARDIZED TESTS COME FROM?

If you've purchased this book, you are probably preparing to apply to college. Part of the long and arduous college admissions process will almost certainly include some standardized tests. For most of you, these tests will come from a company called the College Board. This company has hired the Educational Testing Service, or ETS, to administer and grade their exams.

WHAT IS THE PRINCETON REVIEW?

The Princeton Review is a test-preparation company based in New York City. We have branches all over the United States and abroad. We've developed the techniques you'll find in our books, courses, and online resources by analyzing actual exams and testing their effectiveness with our students.

Tick Tock
We don't waste your time.
We tell you what you
need to know, and, more
important, what you don't
need to know.

Our approach is what makes our techniques unique. We base our principles on the same ones used by the people who write the test. We don't want to waste your time with information that you don't need to know. We know you're busy. We're not going to teach you "How to Appreciate Fine English Literature" (although that's a wonderful thing to know), but rather the information you'll need to get great score improvements on this test. You'll learn to recognize and comprehend the relatively small amount of information that's actually tested. You'll also learn to avoid common traps, to think like the test writers, to find answers to questions of which you're unsure, and to budget your time effectively.

You need to do only three things: trust the techniques, practice them, and practice some more.

WHAT IS THE SAT?

Not an IQ Test
The SAT is not a measure
of your intelligence. It is
a measure only of your
ability to take a standardized test.

The SAT is a three-hour-and-forty-five-minute multiple-choice exam used by colleges to provide a standard measure of high school students around the country. There are three separate scores generated by the SAT: a critical reading score (on a scale of 200–800), a writing score (on a scale of 200–800, which combines separate essay and grammar scores), and a math score (also on a 200–800 scale).

What Does the SAT Measure?

Precious little: some vocabulary, some reading skills, some basic math (sixth-grade through ninth-grade levels). Primarily, it measures your ability to take standardized tests. What it's designed to measure is your ability to perform in college. What it's better at measuring is your gender, race, and family income level. What it's very bad at measuring is your intelligence.

What Are the SAT Subject Tests?

These are a series of one-hour exams administered by ETS. Unlike the SAT, the SAT Subject Tests are designed to measure specific knowledge in specific areas. There are tests in many subject areas, such as biology, history, French, and math. They are each scored separately on the familiar 200–800 scale.

Should I Take the SAT Subject Tests? How Many? When?

About one-third of the colleges that require SAT scores also require that you take two or three SAT Subject Tests. Your first order of business is to start reading those college catalogs. College guidebooks, admissions offices, and guidance counselors should have this information as well.

Do Your Research
You should take SAT Subject Tests only if the schools to which you are applying require them.

How Are the SAT Subject Tests Used by College Admissions?

Some colleges will use SAT Subject Tests to exempt you from requirements. Others will use them to evaluate you. To find out exactly how your college of choice will use these scores, visit the college's website or call its admissions office.

Chapter 2
Approaching the
SAT Subject Tests

Which Test(s) Should I Take? When?

Which test(s) should you take? The answer is simple.

- the SAT Subject Tests that you will do well on
- the tests that the colleges you are applying to require you to take

Some colleges have specific requirements; others do not. Again, start asking questions before you start taking tests. That means you should check with the school's admissions office or website. College guidebooks, catalogs, and guidance counselors should also have this information. Once you find out which, if any, tests are required, part of your decision making is done.

The next step is to find out which of the tests will show your particular strengths. Generally (although, again, check with the colleges you want to apply to) colleges will require (or will "strongly suggest") two SAT Subject Tests: usually Math Level 1 or 2 and something else.

Subject tests are given in the following areas: literature, U.S. history, world history, biology, chemistry, physics, math, and a variety of foreign languages.

Your number one concern is to determine which tests you will score well on. Then you will want to think about the purposes for which the test will be used. If you plan to major in biology, you should probably take the biology test. If you're a whiz at anything, take that test (no, there is no test in video games, pancake eating, or marathon sleeping).

After you've checked your requirements and examined your needs, take a diagnostic test like the ones at the end of this book. See how you do, and with that in mind, determine whether the test is for you.

Try to take the tests as close as possible to the completion of the corresponding coursework you are taking. If you plan to take the SAT Chemistry Subject Test, for example, and you are currently taking high school chemistry, don't postpone the test until next year. Take it while the information is still fresh. (Are you really going to study over the summer? Come on. *Really*?)

When Are the SAT Subject Tests Offered?

In general, you can take from one to three SAT Subject Tests per test date in October, November, December, January, May, and June at test sites across the country. Check the dates carefully, as not all subjects are offered at each administration. You'll want to sit down with a calendar and plan, as there are limited dates and a lot of tests to take. For instance, you may want to retake the SATs on one of those days, or you may want to apply early to a school and have all your scores before your application is due in early fall. Register for the test early so you get the location you want.

An Offer You Can't Refuse
Some schools will "strongly suggest" that you take certain tests. It's wise to follow their suggestions, as they are the ones who will ultimately be judging your application for admission.

Math and More
Typically, schools that require Subject Tests ask you to take either the Math Level 1 or 2 Test, plus another test of your choice.

Don't forget, there are no test dates in February, March, April, July, August, or September.

Should I Take the SAT Literature Subject Test?

The SAT Literature Subject Test will test your knowledge of basic literary terms and your ability to understand and analyze selected literary passages (prose, poetry, and drama) written in English. You don't have to know specifics about literature written in English to do well on the test.

To a Point
Bring only a pencil: You need NO outside knowledge!

If you're unsure about whether you should take this test, start perusing college catalogs or contact the college(s) you will probably be applying to. Admissions offices should be able to tell you if this test is necessary.

Some schools will exempt students from basic English courses if the students achieve high scores. If you feel confident about your ability to analyze and interpret literature, are a good reader, do well in English class, or plan on majoring in English in college, consider taking the SAT Literature Subject Test.

Registration

The easiest way to register is via the Internet at www.collegeboard.com (you'll need a credit card). This site contains other useful information such as the test dates and fees. You can also register by mail (remember regular mail?) by picking up a registration form and Student Bulletin at your guidance counselor's office. If you have any questions, call 866-756-7346. If you need to register for an extension or make special arrangements due to learning differences or disabilities, you can speak with a representative at the College Board by calling 609-771-7137. Start this process early, as the paperwork is fairly extensive.

On test day, you can take a single one-hour test and leave or take two or three different one-hour tests. You may have the scores sent to you, your school, and up to four colleges of your choice. Additional reports can be sent to additional colleges for, yup, additional money. The scores are usually posted online two weeks after the test date and are mailed two weeks later (although they can take up to six weeks to arrive).

What's a Good Score?

It's hard to say exactly what is considered a good score. It depends on the person you're asking. A good score is one that fits into the range of scores received by students usually accepted by the college of your choice. However, if your score falls below the normal range for a certain school, that doesn't mean you shouldn't apply there. A range is a guideline, and schools are often willing to be flexible about what they consider a good score.

What's more important to schools is your percentile ranking (which will be sent along with your scores). This number tells colleges how you fit in with the other people who took the test the same day you did. In other words, a percentile rank of 60 means that 40 percent of test takers scored above you and 60 percent of test takers scored below you. The mean on the SAT Literature Subject Test—and on most SAT Subject Tests—is 600.

Is Any Other Material Available for Practice?

Stay away from the plethora of other test-prep books. The questions in the majority of books on the market bear little, if any, resemblance to actual SAT Subject Test questions. The College Board publishes a book called Real SAT II: Subject Tests, which contains full-length tests for almost all of the SAT Subject Tests offered. You can also go to the College Board's website, www.collegeboard.com, for more information and practice questions.

> For book updates, links to more information, and last-minute test changes, visit this book's online companion at PrincetonReview.com/cracking.

Part II
Cracking the
SAT Literature
Subject Test

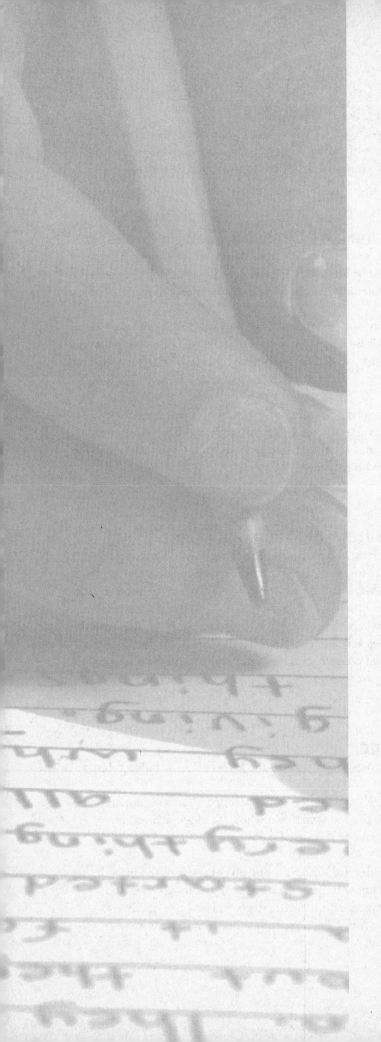

Chapter 3
Overview

In this chapter, you'll learn what the SAT Literature Subject Test comprises and how it's scored. We will tell you how best to use this book and what you can expect from the test.

WHAT DOES THE TEST LOOK LIKE?

You'll have one hour to answer 60 to 63 multiple-choice questions. There will be six to eight reading selections of prose, poetry, or drama, followed by a series of multiple-choice questions. You may be asked to compare two passages.

What Is Tested on the SAT Literature Subject Test?

As with most standardized tests, especially those that are one hour long, the answer is "not much." It would be impossible to test a broad range of topics in so short a time. As a result, the SAT Literature Subject Test is relatively easy to prepare for.

You will be asked to interpret certain excerpts from literature. You will need to be familiar with some of the basic literary terms your teachers have been tossing around in your English classes all these years: Common terms such as *metaphor, tone,* and *imagery* will be covered; obscure terms such as *enjambment* and *metonymy* will not.

DO NOT sit down with a reading list and a dictionary of literary terms (at least, not to prepare for this test). Instead, concentrate on pinning down literary terms that sound vaguely familiar and learning some great techniques for analyzing the types of passages that will be on the exam.

What the SAT Literature Subject Test Doesn't Test

The good news: You're not expected to be familiar with any works of literature; in fact, the test writers try hard to make sure they provide pieces that few students will have read. There's no official reading list for the SAT Literature Subject Test. You won't be asked who the author is, when the piece was written (this information is provided to you), or where the piece fits within the history of literature. In other words, this test requires very little memorization. This is simply a one-hour test of your ability to read and comprehend literature and of your familiarity with basic literary terms.

How to Use This Book

We recommend three simple steps to prepare for the SAT Literature Subject Test.

- Start early. The key to cracking the test is practice. Practicing for six hours the day before the test won't do a whole lot of good (and may fry your brain). Instead, give yourself plenty of time to read this book thoroughly.
- Read this book in order. Inside, you'll find an overview of the information you need to know to get a great score on the test. Terms and techniques are explained, and there are drills and practice questions that ask you to apply them. Each technique builds on a skill we've previously taught you.

- Trust us. We've been in the business for a long time. Some of the techniques may be new to you. They might feel unfamiliar at first, but with practice they will become easier. They may even contradict some things you've learned in English class. Remember that English class is designed to educate you. This book is designed to help you do well on a specific test.

HOW THE TEST IS STRUCTURED

The SAT Literature Subject Test consists of about 60 to 63 multiple-choice questions (the specific number varies on each test). Each of the six to eight passages of prose, poetry, or drama is followed by 4 to 12 questions. Most of the passages come from English and American literature. On occasion, you'll see a passage from another English-speaking culture. All passages are from texts originally written in English—no translations of Cervantes or Baudelaire. Texts may be taken from any time period, but there will be no Middle or Old English on the test (i.e., no *Canterbury Tales* or *Beowulf*).

The breakdown is roughly as follows:

Source
British literature	50%
American literature	50%
Other literature (from Australia, New Zealand, English-speaking Africa, Jamaica, Canada, etc.)	up to 20%

Time Period
Pre-Eighteenth century	30%
Eighteenth and Nineteenth centuries	30%
Twentieth and Twenty-first centuries	40%

Genre
Prose (2–4 passages)	50%
Poetry (2–4 passages)	50%
Other (usually drama)	20%

HOW THE TEST IS SCORED

The SAT Literature Subject Test is scored like the SAT and all other SAT Subject Tests. You get a raw score based on the following formula:

> 1 point for each correct answer
>
> $-\dfrac{1}{4}$ (number of wrong answers)
>
> = raw score

Blank answers neither add nor take away from the raw score. Test administrators then calculate what each score corresponds to on a scale from 200–800, which gives you the familiar "out of 800" score you're used to.

For the most part, every raw point translates to approximately 10 points on the scaled score.

Summary

Did you get all that?

- Common terms will be tested; obscure terms will not.

- You don't need any outside knowledge of literature.

- Start studying early.

- You get one raw point for a correct answer and $-\dfrac{1}{4}$ point for each wrong answer.

Chapter 4
Test Strategies

In this chapter, you'll learn some general test strategies, including how and when to guess, the power of Process of Elimination, getting rid of careless errors, how to use your score sheet, and the order in which you should attack the questions.

TEST STRATEGIES

The Princeton Review has developed effective and time-saving strategies to optimize your study time and improve your score. Some of the strategies will be unfamiliar at first, or you may not be convinced that they'll work. But give them a try—our methods have improved thousands of scores.

You may have heard that you get penalized for guessing on the New SAT and the SAT Subject Tests. This is only partly true. The test administrators dock you $\frac{1}{4}$ of a point for wrong answers, but that doesn't mean you should leave an answer blank if you absolutely aren't 100 percent sure it's correct.

Eliminate and Guess

If this worries you, let's say you must take "educated guesses." That sounds like an intelligent plan. How does this benefit you?

You may be tempted to leave blanks when you don't know the answers, but a little examination of ETS's scoring system should convince you to blacken those ovals a bit more frequently than you have in the past.

Let's say that when the test begins, you have the overwhelming urge to take a nap. You put your head down on the desk and close your eyes, only to awaken when the proctor announces that there are five minutes remaining in the test. Wiping the drool from the side of your mouth, you decide to take your chances and fill in the same letter all the way down. In a statistically perfect world, you would probably get about one in five questions correct (and the Chicago Cubs would occasionally win the World Series).

Here's why.

$$12 \text{ right} = 12 \text{ points}$$
$$48 \text{ wrong} = \frac{1}{4} \text{ point off for every wrong answer} = \frac{48}{4} = 12$$
$$\text{Number right} - \text{number wrong} = 12 - 12 = 0$$

$$0 \text{ works out to a scaled score of } 300.$$

So ETS has achieved its goal—a monkey (or a nap-prone student) trained to fill in choice (C) all the way down the page gets a score of 300. The point is: You're not penalized for making random guesses. In fact, nothing happens when you guess.

Now let's say you wake up from your nap and have enough time to eliminate one obviously wrong answer to each question (never mind logistics, we're doing statistics here). With one sucky answer gone, you now have a one-in-four chance of getting the answer right.

So out of 60 questions you get:

$$15 \text{ right} = 15 \text{ points}$$

$$45 \text{ wrong} = \frac{1}{4} \text{ point off for every wrong answer} = \frac{45}{4} = 11.25$$

$$\text{Number right} - \text{number wrong} = 15 - 11.25 = 3.75$$

$$3.75 \text{ works out to a scaled score of } 340.$$

This score will not get you to the Ivy League, but remember, every extra point earns you approximately 10 points on the scaled score. In other words, if you get one right and then three wrong, you're still up a quarter of a point. Four of those earns you one whole extra point.

Did we lose you on the math stuff? After all, we're supposed to be studying for the SAT Literature Subject Test, right? It all boils down to this: ANY TIME YOU CAN ELIMINATE EVEN ONE WRONG ANSWER, YOU MUST GUESS, even if the other answers don't make any sense to you at all. It's mathematically proven.

Don't Rush

Some students think they need to finish every question to get a good score on the SAT Literature Subject Test. Not at all. Don't be afraid to skip a few questions as you go along. You don't get any more points for answering hard questions than you do for answering easy ones, so there's no reason to bust your, well, you know. If you race through the test, you run the risk of making careless errors, misreading questions, or not choosing the right answers, when spending just a little more time on the questions would have gotten you those crucial extra points instead of those quarter-points off.

On the flipside, you don't want to linger on any one question for too long. Don't get bogged down by one complicated or difficult question. It only takes away from time you can use to answer easier questions. If you come across a stumper, eliminate obviously wrong answers and take an educated guess. If you really can't eliminate anything, skip it completely. Move on to a question that you know you can get right.

Since the questions are not in order of difficulty, it is up to you to decide which questions look hard and which look easy. Go ahead and judge a book by its cover. If the question looks hard to you, reminds you of an unpleasant childhood experience, or nauseates you, skip it. You can always return to it if you have time.

In other words, pace yourself. Don't go too fast or too slow. Consult this handy chart to see how many questions you can leave blank and still get the score you want.

No Loitering
Don't linger too long on any one question—it's worth only one point!

Scoring Chart

Scaled Score	Raw Score	# of Questions to Do	# Wrong	Percentile
800	56–61	all	4	99+
750–790	50–55	58–60	6	95–99
700–740	45–49	53–55	6	82–94
650–690	39–43	49–52	8	66–81
600–640	33–38	43–48	8	49–65
550–590	28–32	38–42	8	33–48
500–540	23–27	36–39	10	21–32
400–490	11–22	24–34	10	1–20
300–390	1–10	18–28	15	< 1

MAY I TAKE YOUR ORDER?

Let's review so far: Slow down, and guess more aggressively. To this, we'll add a third mandate.

Don't Panic

You are taking the test—the test is not taking you. You have 60 minutes to take this exam. So don't waste time on a passage you hate and then never get to a really great passage you would have loved tackling (love, of course, being a relative term—we understand it's a standardized test). Think about the types of passages you like and those on which you tend to score highest. If poetry is the first passage on the test, and poetry is your weak area, move on to a selection you feel more comfortable with and come back to the poetry passage later. You'll get that all-important boost of confidence right away. Sixty minutes is not a long time (although it's the entire life span of some insects). It's a sprint, not a marathon. Try to hit your stride in the first five minutes, not halfway through.

Decide in which order you want to tackle the passages. Is prose, poetry, or drama your strong suit? Are you more comfortable with contemporary passages, or do you like older themes? Do you appreciate the sparseness of poetry? The flow of prose? Poems about nature? Excerpts from stories? Knowing what you're good at will help you choose which questions to do as you come to them and which questions to shelve until later. For example, if you're a slow reader, get shorter passages out of the way first.

At this point, decide what kinds of questions you want to do. There's no law that says you have to go in order. Skip Roman numeral questions until later (more on these in Chapter 5). If you come across a word you're not familiar with, save that question for later; do something that's easy instead. There's bound to be something that looks a little better. Nothing feels better than getting questions right at the start. If you meet more challenging questions later in the test, who cares? You're allowed to leave some blank anyway.

Once you've decided which questions to do, how do you go about getting the answers right? The following is a discussion of general strategies for multiple-choice tests. Feel free to apply these techniques to other standardized tests you may take.

PROCESS OF ELIMINATION (POE)

Process of Elimination (POE) is your weapon of mass destruction, if you will. If you're good at POE, you never have to know the right answer to a question. You just have to be able to identify the wrong answers. For example:

> 3. Lines 4–7 of the poem are a good example of
>
>   (A) French cheese
>   (B) tap-dancing shoes
>   (C) prize-winning barbecue technology
>   (D) clean socks
>   (E) synecdochical symbolism

Although slightly silly, the question illustrates the idea: If you know what the answer can't be, you are left with the correct answer by default. (Don't worry; you don't have to know what "synecdochical" is.)

Cross Out Wrong Answers

This may seem too obvious for words, but it's extremely important. A lot of students get lazy and just read down the list until they get to an answer they like. Don't be this student. In your test booklet (not your answer sheet!), put a line through the letter of each answer you eliminate. Get into this habit early, so it will be second nature to you by the time the test date rolls around. Imagine yourself at the end of this test. It is your third test today. You're very tired. Your brain is reeling. It would be easy to make a mistake and pick an answer you've already eliminated or fall for a trick answer in the same way that vulnerable kids get persuaded to join the wrong crowd. So put lines through the letters of the answer choices you've eliminated, and don't give in to peer pressure.

If an answer is clearly wrong, cross it out. If you have no clue what is meant by an answer choice, put a question mark (?) next to the letter. If you like an answer, put a check mark (✔) next to it. If you really like it, put two check marks (✔✔).

Thus, a sample answer set might look like this:

✓   (A) I like this answer.
       (B) This answer is wrong.
?   (C) I don't understand this answer.
       (D) This answer is wrong.
✓✓   (E) I really love this answer.

Once you've cleared the proverbial air of bad answers, you can make an educated guess among the choices that are left.

AVOID BONEHEADED ANSWERS

Boneheaded answers are those that ETS puts into the answer choices to try to trick you. They look like great answers because ETS thinks it knows how you think and teases you with an answer that off the top of your head might look right. On hard questions, be suspicious of easy answers. Look for a trick. Here's an example:

24. As it is used in the passage, the word "rare"
(line 22) means

    (A) uncommon
    (B) rude
    (C) exaggerated
    (D) undercooked
    (E) irrelevant

A boneheaded test taker would see the word "rare" and, knowing it means "under-cooked," pick (D). But think: The question begins with the words "As it is used in this passage . . ." This is not a vocabulary test; it's a test of reading and interpreting literature. Even if you've never seen the word "rare" before, you will probably be able to tell its meaning from the context. Without the passage in front of you now it'll be hard to figure out, but the correct answer is (A), "uncommon," a secondary definition of "rare."

A WORD (OR SEVERAL) ON BUBBLING

Bubbling is the art of transferring your answers onto the score sheet. When you bubble, be sure to fill in the oval completely so that the computer can give you the credit you deserve. When skipping around, pay special attention to where you bubble. It is a horrible feeling to get to question 55 and realize you've just bubbled the answer for 54. It's like misbuttoning your shirt, only worse.

There are two methods you can use to ensure you're bubbling in the right place. Pick one, and stick with it, and you'll never get lost bubbling again.

Method 1: The Rat Pack

Bubble the answers to each passage. Answer all the questions for one passage in the test booklet by circling the letter. Save up your answers, and every time you get to the end of a passage, transfer your answers to the bubbles on the score sheet.

Method 2: The Worry Wart

Answer questions directly on the bubble sheet. Every time you do a multiple of ten, check back to make sure that your answers correspond to the questions you did. Then you'll never be more than ten questions out of whack. This method takes more of your precious time, but if you're prone to misbuttoning your shirt, or making bubbling mistakes, use this.

It doesn't matter which method you use, as long as you pick one and stay with it. It's important to have a reliable system in place BEFORE test day.

SKIPPING QUESTIONS

Skip to Your Lou
Be ready to skip questions!

Unlike the SAT or the Math Level 1 and Level 2 Subject Tests, the SAT Literature Subject Test does not pretend to get harder as the question numbers rise. That means that a hard question is one that's tough for you and that an easy question is one that's not so challenging. This is called your "Personal Order of Difficulty" (POOD). On the test, you should plan on going through the entire test at least twice. The first time, do the questions that are easy and medium-hard for you. Skip the ones that seem difficult. Make sure you circle the hard questions very obviously in your test booklet so you remember to go back to them.

On the second pass, do the questions you skipped the first time. If you want, you can do three or four passes, but don't spend too much time deciding on the difficulty level of a question. You should be able to tell within a second or two.

> **Shirk Work**
> Each test has at least ten questions that 60 percent of students get wrong. Don't bother with these questions unless you have extra time—they're not worth it.

You can also do multiple passes within a passage. Sometimes doing the fifth or sixth question in a passage gives you a better idea of what the second question in the passage is asking. We'll talk more about this in Chapter 5.

Don't neglect to keep track of your time. Look at how many questions there are for each passage. If you're trying to decide between two passages at the end, you might want to opt for the one with more questions so you don't have to read two passages. Or you may opt for the passage that has easier questions (usually specific or line-reference questions, not general or reasoning questions).

Summary

Did you get all that?

o   Slow down.

o   Don't panic.

o   Use Process of Elimination (POE).

o   Take educated guesses.

o   Avoid boneheaded answers.

o   Bubble wisely—pick a bubbling method, and stick to it.

o   Look through the passages, and pick the ones you'll do first.

o   Decide on a POOD (Personal Order of Difficulty).

o   Make two or three passes.

Chapter 5
Test Strategies for the SAT Literature Subject Test

This chapter familiarizes you with each type of question that appears on the test and with the best strategies to answer specific, general, and weird questions correctly.

LOOK FAMILIAR?

You may have noticed that the SAT Literature Subject Test bears a startling resemblance to the Critical Reading section of the SAT. This is a good thing—this means you are familiar with the test format. The main difference between the SAT Critical Reading section and the SAT Literature Subject Test is that the latter does not test vocabulary in the same way as the SAT (except for literary terms—we'll get to those in Chapter 6). More good news: There is a greater emphasis on inference and interpretation questions on the SAT Literature Subject Test. This means that the answers you need are in the passage. They may be buried or confusingly worded, but they are in there. So the SAT Literature Subject Test is like an open-book exam.

There's No Right or Wrong
Look for the best answer, not the right answer.

It's important to remember that often you won't see an answer you love. That's okay. You're not necessarily looking for the "right" answer; the interpretation of literature is subjective. What you are looking for is the answer that stinks the least. The "least worst" answer is the one you want. If you remember this, you'll find yourself a lot less frustrated. There's bound to be one answer choice that's better than the others, and that will be the correct response to the question.

APPROACH THE QUESTIONS THE WAY YOU WOULD CRITICAL READING

1. Look at the date. Is the passage modern or old? If you recognize the passage, try to recall what you know about the author. For instance, you may recognize the passage as part of a Dickens novel. Even if you don't remember what the novel was about, you remember that Dickens wrote a lot about the plight of the urban poor in nineteenth-century England. Any answer that talks about overseas trade or farming is not going to be correct. Similarly, classical literature usually explores themes of love, love lost, beauty, or death. Modern passages are more likely to be about racism, coming of age, individual rights, or technology.

2. Next, read the passage. You don't have to study it carefully; just read enough to know what is basically going on in the passage. Remember, you can (and must) go back to the passage when you answer the questions, so you're just reading to get a sense of where to find the answer when it comes time to search for it. You should read just closely enough so that you can summarize the main theme and tone.

3. The third step is to decide which question to do first. Questions come in three types: **specific questions** (line-reference, almost-line-

> **Theme and Tone**
> **Theme** is a unifying idea that is a recurrent element in a literary or artistic work. One of Shakespeare's favorite themes is unrequited love.
>
> **Tone** is the manner of expression, the quality or sound of a person's voice or writing. For example, *The Adventures of Huckleberry Finn* is written in a very humorous and informal tone.

reference, and vocabulary-in-context questions), **general questions**, and **weird questions**.

4. Once you've decided which question to do, cover the answer choices. Literally. Use your hand to hide the choices. Then you know you won't be tempted by the wrong one until you've formulated your answer.

5. Questions are usually worded in ETS-speak. That means they have extra words or a complicated structure to confuse you. Get rid of this verbiage by translating the question into your own words.

6. Go back to the passage. Always go back to the passage to find the answer to the question. Don't rely on your memory of the passage; make sure you can point to the answer in the text.

7. Find the answer and put it in your own words. If you don't use your own words, you won't know exactly what you're looking for in the answer choices. When you've got the answer in your own words, turn to the answer choices and look for a match.

8. Use Process of Elimination (POE). Get rid of bad answers—answers that don't match YOUR answer. Once you've eliminated the wrong answers, you're left with the right one!

You're the Man/Woman
Use your own words to answer the question.

Specific Questions

Line-Reference Questions
Specific questions generally take the least time. They usually give a specific line reference for you to find. Read a few lines above and below the reference in the passage, and answer the question IN YOUR OWN WORDS.

Drill #1

Here are some examples of line-reference questions. Try putting the questions in your own words. We've done the first one for you.

14. The main character refers to her father as "the distant shadow" (line 7) in order to

Why does the main character call her father "the distant shadow"?

24. In describing the response of the "careless birds" (line 10) to the "venerable hunter" (line 14), the author suggests that they

Why do the "careless birds" respond to the "venerable hunter"?

49. The idea behind Joseph's "grand caper" (line 14) is to prove that

What is the point of the "grand caper"?

30. In context, the meaning of the word "favored" (line 20) is closest to

What does "favored" mean in line 20?

Answers can be found on page 106.

The reason that these questions often take less time to answer than others is that they tell you exactly where to look for the answer. Generally, specific questions are in chronological order, so that a question about line 4 will come before a question about line 17.

Almost-Line-Reference Questions

Sometimes questions are line-reference questions in disguise. They don't mention a specific line number but nonetheless offer clues as to where you can find the answer. Usually there's one word or phrase that will help:

> 13.   The author mentions *Vanity Fair* in order to

Here, just scan the text for the words *Vanity Fair* (conveniently italicized). Then read five lines above and five lines below for the context.

> 58.   Sue Anne considers the Bali tariffs unfair because

Now you'll have to scan the text for the words "Sue Anne" or "Bali" or "tariffs." Other than the fact that no line number is given, this question is still a line-reference question, and the answer should be relatively easy to locate in the passage.

Vocabulary-in-Context Questions

Vocabulary-in-context questions ask you what a word means. This will almost always test a secondary or tertiary (third) meaning of a word or a word that has changed meaning since the original text was written.

If you come across one of these questions, go back to the text and cross out the word. Then write in your own word for the word you're being tested on. Go through the answer choices, and pick the one that best matches your word.

Don't boneheadedly go directly to the answer choices and choose a synonym for the word in the question. That will most likely generate the wrong answer.

Here's a vocabulary-in-context question borrowed from the previous page:

> In context, the meaning of the word "favored" (line 20) is closest to

First, translate the question: What does "favored" mean?

Return to the passage. Line 20 says, "Clearly Amahl favored his father; it was almost as though his mother was not involved in his birth." Read a few lines above and below to make sure you get the context. Cross out the word "favor." Replace it with something like "looked like." Now go through the answer choices:

- (A)   resembled
- (B)   presented
- (C)   was partial to
- (D)   prioritized
- (E)   supported

Choice (A) best matches the words we supplied, so it is the correct answer. (Note that the word "favored" usually means "supported"—a wrong answer!)

General Questions

Point It Out
Make sure you can point to the answer in the text.

General questions ask about the theme or structure, tone, or style of the piece as a whole. They may or may not ask a question about the attitude of a character, the author, or the author's intentions. Pick an answer only if you can point to the specific place in the text that supports your answer. (If your justification is "I don't know where, but I feel like it's in there," you're probably not choosing the right answer, or you need to look harder in the text.)

If you answer these questions after you answer specific questions, you should have a good idea of what the passage is about—you may not even have to go back to the text. Don't worry if you need to consult the passage, however. That's what it's there for.

Kissing Cousins
Watch out for the difference between theme and structure.

One trick to watch out for is the old theme-versus-structure question. Theme questions ask about what the passage is trying to say. Structure questions ask about how it's being said.

Some theme questions:

2. The primary theme of the poem is

16. The passage is primarily concerned with

34. Mr. Beetlegeuse's attitude in the passage can best be described as

Some structure questions:

12. The structure of the narrative can best be described as

55. The author uses incomplete sentences most likely to

60. The two stanzas are most different in that they

Don't try to answer a structure question with a theme answer.

The procedure for approaching general questions is the same as for specific ones: Translate the question, find the answer in the passage, put the answer in your own words, and use POE.

Weird Questions

Weird questions come in two flavors: NOT/LEAST/EXCEPT and Roman numeral. They are usually (although not always) harder than other types of questions. They are also considered time suckers and are best skipped. Glance at them to see if they are easy or hard, and don't be afraid to come back to them at the end or leave them blank.

NOT/LEAST/EXCEPT Questions

Whenever you see a NOT/LEAST/EXCEPT question, circle the word that is capitalized so you don't forget that this question is inside out. Instead of finding one right answer, you are looking for the one wrong answer. Avoid careless errors by writing a "Y" for "Yes" next to each answer choice that is correct, and an "N" for "No" next to the ones that are incorrect. You should end up with four of one letter and one of the other. That one is the right answer.

For example:

> 22. All of the following are true of bunny rabbits EXCEPT
>
>   Y (A) They have four legs
>   Y (B) They are soft
>   Y (C) They eat carrots
>   N (D) They have wings
>   Y (E) They have long ears

Because answer choice (D) is the only "N," it is the correct answer.

Roman Numeral Questions

Roman numeral questions are three questions rolled into one. Here's an example:

> 23. The author suggests that bunny rabbits are
>   I. Good pets
>   II. Yxzmkls
>   III. Smaller than most dogs
>
>   (A) I only
>   (B) II only
>   (C) III only
>   (D) I and III only
>   (E) II and III only

Go through your options one by one. It's not a bad idea to begin with the Roman numeral that appears most frequently or with the one you know is true. In this case, you know that rabbits are good pets because you've read the passage. So Roman numeral I has to be in the answer. Right away you can get rid of (B), (C), and (E) because they don't contain "I." Now, be smart. The only choices that are left involve I and III. All you have to do is see if III is true. Don't even worry about II (good news, because you don't know what Yxzmkls means). So go back to the passage and see if bunnies are smaller than most dogs. They are. Choice (D) is the correct answer.

If you do this carefully, you can avoid doing extra work. You may not need to try every Roman numeral, just a couple of them. This will save you time and effort.

Drill #2

Make sure you can answer the following questions before you move on.

What are the eight steps for tackling questions?

1. Look at the date.
2. Read the passage.
3. Decide which questions to do first.
4. Literally cover the answers.
5. Translate the question.
6. Refer back to the passage.
7. Put answers in own words.
8. POE

What are the three kinds of questions on the SAT Literature Subject Test?

1. line reference
2. almost-line reference
3. vocabulary-in-context

What are the two kinds of weird questions on the SAT Literature Subject Test?

1. NOT/LEAST/EXCEPT
2. Roman Numeral

Answers can be found on page 106.

Summary

Make sure you can

o   differentiate between specific and general questions

o   identify the type of question: line reference, almost line reference, vocabulary in context, general, NOT/LEAST/EXCEPT, and Roman numeral questions

o   quickly decide which questions to do first

o   handle weird questions

Chapter 6
Terms—The Only Stuff You Need to Know

This chapter covers everything you need to know for the test. Yup, that's it. Some of the terms will be familiar to you; others may be new, but you can use them all in English class afterward. Practice drills are included for you to test your knowledge, and a list of what ETS says it's testing you on—which bears little or no resemblance to the actual test—wraps it all up!

INTRODUCTION TO ANALYZING POETRY, PROSE, AND DRAMA

Flavors
Passages on the SAT Literature Subject Test will be poetry, prose, or drama.

The SAT Literature Subject Test doesn't review your knowledge of literature in general, but there are some terms that are helpful to know. To begin, let's define the following categories:

POETRY: A poem is a rhythmic expression of feelings or ideas, kind of like the lyrics to a song. It may or it may not rhyme.

PROSE: This one's easy—if it's not poetry, it's prose. Prose is generally broken down into two categories: fiction and nonfiction.

DRAMA: A play; something that is intended to be acted out. Plays can be written in verse or in a more conversational style.

LITERARY TERMS YOU NEED TO KNOW

Learn This
Become familiar with the basic literary terms listed here.

Here's a list of the basics. Each is followed by examples or a discussion of what it is. If you're familiar with the term, move on. Concentrate on any that are unfamiliar to you or that you feel you could use some work on. Make flash cards to help you memorize these terms.

ALLEGORY: A story with underlying symbols that really represent something else. A character can be allegorical.

> Example: The nursery rhyme "Humpty Dumpty" was really a political allegory in which the characters represented people in government who were falling from power.

ALLITERATION: The use of a repeated consonant sound, usually at the beginning of a series of words.

> Examples: *Silently stalking her sister on the stairs . . . Falling, falling, fearfully falling . . .*

ALLUSION: A reference to something or someone, usually literary.

> Example: Mr. Jones got the neighborhood kids to do his yard work—just as Tom Sawyer got the kids to paint the fence.

ANACHRONISM: Placing a person or object in an inappropriate historical situation. It can be deliberate or unintentional.

> Example: George Washington rode his limousine downtown for the inauguration.

ANALOGY: Comparing something to something else.

> Example: Starting a new job is like starting a new school year.

ANECDOTE: A short narrative, story, or tale.

ANTAGONIST: The major character opposing the protagonist. Usually the villain.

> Example: Boris Badanov, Bullwinkle's enemy, is my favorite antagonist.

ANTHROPOMORPHISM: Assigning human attributes such as emotions or physical characteristics to nonhuman things. Used almost exclusively for attributing human characteristics to animals.

> Examples: My cat, Fluffy, is always so happy to see me.
> The mother rhinoceros was depressed for weeks over the loss of her offspring to the cruel hunter.

DICTION: Choice of words. Diction can be incorrect if the wrong word is used. It can be stilted or flowery. It can set the tone. Choice of words can be important. Wrong words can be used to indicate a character's ignorance or humor. Flowery words can reveal a character's pretension.

FABLE: A story that has a moral, usually involving animals as the main characters.

> Example: Aesop's fable about the grasshopper and the ant is a great illustration of why you should work hard and prepare for bad times.

FIGURATIVE LANGUAGE: Language characterized by figures of speech such as metaphors and similes as well as elaborate expression through imagery.

HYPERBOLE: A deliberate exaggeration.

> Examples: Taking that test was the easiest thing I've ever done.
> There were a billion people at the concert.
> I'm going to be grounded for ten years when my parents find out where I was last night.
> The new teacher gave us fifty hours of homework for tonight.

IRONY: An expression of meaning that is the opposite of the literal meaning.

> Example: The music is so loud that I can hardly hear it.

Stories can be ironic as well when they end in a way that is the opposite of what you would have expected. A story about an obsessively clean man who is killed by a garbage truck is ironic. O. Henry's classic story "The Gift of the Magi" is a great example of irony. The husband sells his watch to buy his wife an ornate hair comb for Christmas, only to find out that she has sold her hair to buy him a watch chain.

METAPHOR: A metaphor is a comparison like a simile, but it doesn't use the words "like" or "as." It's a little more subtle. It's important to note, however, that in literary criticism, the word "metaphor" is frequently used when, strictly speaking, the term "simile" applies. Don't be confused if you are asked if the writer is using metaphor and you see the words "like" or "as."

> Examples: She was a breath of fresh air in the classroom.
> The new principal was more strict than a prison warden.
> Johnny is a tiger when it comes to football.

METER: The rhythm of a poem. The most common meter is iambic (like a horse galloping: "I wish I were an Oscar Meyer weiner"—duh DUH duh DUH duh DUH duh DUH duh DUH).

NARRATIVE: A literary representation of an event or a story—the text itself.

ONOMATOPOEIA: A word intended to simulate the actual sound of the thing or action it describes.

> Examples: A *buzzing* bee.
> "*Bam!*" The superhero hit the criminal.
> The snake *hissed* at its predator.

OXYMORON: A phrase in which the words are contradictory.

> Examples: He was happy in his pessimism.
> They were intelligently ignorant.

Sometimes an oxymoron is used for comic effect; sometimes it is used to illustrate a paradox.

PARABLE: A story that has a moral. The story of the Good Samaritan is a famous parable from the Bible.

PARADOX: This is a phrase that appears to be contradictory but that actually contains some basic truth that resolves the apparent contradiction.

> Example: Although he was sentenced to ten years of hard labor, the guilt-ridden criminal looked as though a weight had been lifted from his shoulders.

PARALLELISM: The repetition of sounds, meanings, or structures to create a certain style.

> Example: I don't want your pity. I don't want your money. I don't want your car. I want only your love.

PARODY: A literary work in which the style of an author is imitated for comic effect or ridicule.

PASTORAL: A work that deals with the lives of people, especially shepherds, in the country or in nature (as opposed to people in the city).

PATHOS: Something that evokes a feeling of pity or sympathy. Think of the word "pathetic." A pathetic person adds an element of pathos to a story.

> Example: And so, the little orphan girl curled up on the cold steps of the church and tried to sleep.

PERSONIFICATION: Assigning human attributes to something nonhuman.

> Examples: I hope that fortune will smile on me when I take my exam. My car always seems so miserable when I let someone else drive.

PERSPECTIVE: The place from which the narrator or character sees things.

> Example: From my perspective, what you did was horrible, although others might not think so.

POINT OF VIEW: The perspective from which a story is presented to a reader. The most common points of view are first person and third person (more on this in Chapter 7).

PROTAGONIST: The main character, usually the hero.

> Example: Jane Eyre, Charlotte Brontë's most famous protagonist, is my favorite heroine in English literature.

SATIRE: Ridicule of a subject. *Saturday Night Live* often makes use of satire. When the cast pokes fun at the president, they are satirizing the politics of the country. Satire is humorous and often intended to point out something about a serious subject.

SIMILE: A simile is a comparison of two things using the words "like" or "as."

> Examples: I'm as quick as a cricket.
> He's as sly as a fox.
> She was greeted like a rooster in a hen house.

Similes are frequently used in poetry to evoke an idea through an image.

STANZA: The divisions in a poem, like a paragraph in prose.

STYLE: The author's unique manner of expression; the author's voice.

> Example: I'm not a fan of that author; his style is too long-winded and flowery.

THEME: The main idea of a piece of literature.

TONE: Style or manner of expression.

> Example: Funeral eulogies have a somber tone.

Parts of Speech

Although you don't need to be able to diagram sentences, sometimes questions ask you about how words function within a text. This may already be old-hat for you. If so, smile smugly as you review parts of speech:

Noun   a person, place, thing, or idea; usually the subject of the sentence

Verb   action word or a word that expresses a state of being

Adverb   modifies (describes, refers to) a verb, an adjective, or another adverb

Adjective description word that modifies a noun

Pronoun   word that takes the place of a noun

In the sentence, "The quick, brown fox jumped gracefully over the lazy dog,"

- *quick, brown,* and *lazy* are **adjectives** (they modify *fox* and *dog*)
- *fox* is a **noun** and the **subject** of the sentence; *dog* is also a **noun**
- *jumped* is a **verb**
- *gracefully* is an **adverb** (it modifies the verb *jumped*)

Drill #1

The sentences below contain examples of simile, metaphor, and personification/anthropomorphism. Identify the literary device used in each sentence and place the sentence number in the appropriate column in the chart.

Metaphor	Simile	Personification/Anthropomorphism
4	1	2
7	3	5
9	8	6
		10

1. She moved through the room like a cool summer breeze.
2. The house shivered in the cold winter wind.
3. Marie was as sad as a basset hound when she heard the news.
4. The news that she had won the sweepstakes was a dream come true to Mary Anne.
5. Bunnies often feel dejected when kept in their hutches for too long.
6. The wind sang a song of melancholy as it whistled through the field.
7. Taking standardized tests is torture unless you're prepared.
8. Like a soldier marching into battle, the student body president went to meet with the new principal.
9. That test was no day at the beach.
10. My puppy is too proud to wear a silly collar like that one!

Answers can be found on page 107.

Drill #2

The sentences below contain examples of onomatopoeia, alliteration, oxymoron, and pathos. Identify the literary device used in each sentence and place the sentence number in the appropriate column in the chart.

Onomatopoeia	Alliteration	Oxymoron	Pathos
____	____	____	____
____	____	____	____
____	____	____	____
____	____	____	____
____	____	____	____

1. Yet again they made fun of the poor handicapped boy because he was too short to reach the sink.
2. The hissing of the snake alerted the hikers to the possible danger within the cave.
3. He was conspicuous by his absence at the new student meeting.
4. Sailing swiftly through the water, they won the race.
5. Napoleon was a giant in his smallness.
6. After waiting all through the night, Joan and David were told that no more petitions would be accepted, and their request for medicine for their sick child would go unheard.
7. "Knock, knock, knock" was tapped out to signal that a club member was at the door.
8. The new attorney on the case was practically pompous.
9. An odd atmosphere descended on the room, perfectly described by Shakespeare's "heavy lightness."

Answers can be found on page 107.

Drill #3

Test yourself: See if you can define the following terms. Check your answers in the glossary of terms on pages 38–42.

allegory _____

satire _____

parable _____

protagonist _____

stanza _____

parallelism _____

perspective _____

Drill #4

Read the following poem carefully before you choose your answers.

"Elegy"

Let them bury your big eyes
In the secret earth securely,
Your thin fingers, and your fair,
Soft, indefinite-coloured hair,—
5   All of these in some way, surely,
From the secret earth shall rise;
Not for these I sit and stare,
Broken and bereft completely:
Your young flesh that sat so neatly
10   On your little bones will sweetly
Blossom in the air.

But your voice . . . never the rushing
Of a river underground,
Not the rising of the wind
15   In the trees before the rain,
Not the woodcock's watery call,
Not the note the white-throat utters,
Not the feet of children pushing
Yellow leaves along the gutters
20   In the blue and bitter fall,
Shall content my musing mind
For the beauty of that sound
That in no new way at all
Ever will be heard again.

25   Sweetly through the sappy stalk
Of the vigourous weed,
Holding all it held before,
Cherished by the faithful sun,
On and on eternally
30   Shall your altered fluid run,
Bud and bloom and go to seed:
But your singing days are done;
But the music of your talk
Never shall the chemistry
35   Of the secret earth restore.
All your lovely words are spoken.
Once the ivory box is broken,
Beats the golden bird no more.

(1927)

1. The main verb in the second stanza is

   (A) rising (line 14)
   (B) pushing (line 18)
   (C) fall (line 20)
   (D) shall content (line 21)
   (E) will be heard (line 24)

2. The "voice" of the deceased is compared to all of the following EXCEPT

   (A) the sound of an underground stream
   (B) the wind
   (C) the woodcock
   (D) the music of a bird
   (E) the pattering of feet

3. The phrase "cherished by the faithful sun" (line 28) is an example of

   (A) irony
   (B) paradox
   (C) personification
   (D) oxymoron
   (E) poetic license

4. The poem is written in

   (A) a regular meter
   (B) the elegiac tradition
   (C) a consistent rhyme scheme
   (D) an extended allegory
   (E) pathetic empathy

Answers can be found on pages 107–108.

WHAT ETS SAYS IT'S TESTING YOU ON

ETS lists six categories on its website from which test writers draw their questions. Although it's not important for you to memorize these, a short discussion of their meanings should help clarify what will be on the test.

1. Meaning

Of course, the biggest thing that ETS will test you on is the meaning of the passage, especially if it's completely obscure. Many questions will be devoted to seeing if you understand the plot and motivation of the characters. If the passage is persuasive, the test writers will want to see if you understand the argument. Also, the test will ask you for the meanings of words in context. You can expect that a secondary or tertiary (third) definition of the word will apply. The word's meaning depends upon the words that surround it. Make sure you look for its meaning in the passage. Never assume a definition without considering its context.

2. Form

Although you won't have to tell a sonnet from a sestina, you might have to judge whether the passage is a fable, allegory, etc. Also, the test will ask you about the structure of the passage. Is it chronological? Does it follow the development of an argument? How does the author manage the transitions from one paragraph or stanza to the next? Organization is also an important topic—you might be called upon to explain how the passage is arranged.

3. Tone

Tone is a blanket term for how the passage sounds. Diction questions will test you on the author's choice of words. Is it high-falutin' or fairly lowbrow? Does it sound like how people talk today, or does it sound more like a historical movie? A question about syntax will ask how the words fit together or whether the sentences are long-winded or short and abrupt. Finally, emphasis questions will test you on what is and is not important in the passage.

4. Figurative Language

Questions that ask about figurative language will test you on your ability to perceive similes, metaphors, expression, and descriptive language.

5. Narrative Voice

Similar to tone, narrative voice is how the narrator sounds in the passage. Who is doing the talking? How does he/she talk? Does he/she use slang or proper English? Don't forget that the author, narrator, and characters are sometimes three different entities. Unless the passage is an autobiography, assume that the opinions expressed are those of a narrator that the author has created, not the author's own opinions.

6. Characterization

This is a less frequently explored topic on the SAT Literature Subject Test. Characterization refers to how the author represents his or her character(s) in the piece. Sometimes authors describe their characters. Sometimes they let the characters speak for themselves. Sometimes authors let us hear about a character from other characters in the text. Characterization questions ask about the ways in which you learn about how a character thinks and acts.

Again, you don't have to memorize these six areas. They are just supplied so that you can keep them in mind as you read the passage, to have an idea of what ETS wants to test you on.

Summary

Did you get all that?

Before moving on, you should be comfortable identifying

- prose

- poetry

- drama

- the literary terms on pages 38–42

- parts of speech

Chapter 7
Analyzing Prose

This chapter covers characters, tense, and point of view, focusing on the two main kinds of prose you need to be familiar with: fiction and nonfiction. By the end of this chapter, you should understand genre, character, and voice.

WHAT IS PROSE?

Prose is often described as everything that is not poetry. But this definition does not give prose enough credit. Prose is writing that does not have strict metrical rhythm. It's how people speak; it's the stuff of novels and speeches and essays and chronicles, comic books, pamphlets, tracts, newspaper articles, letters, dissertation... (you get the point).

Prose is generally comprised of two categories: fiction and nonfiction. For the purposes of this test, it's useless to distinguish between the two, as you'll never have to decide if something is invented (fiction) or factual (nonfiction).

Tense

Back in the Day
Most writers use the past tense, even if the action of the story takes place in the past, present, or future.

Most prose takes place in the past. It's how we naturally tell a story. After all, we usually talk about things that have already happened ("Oh my God, did I tell you what happened to me at the mall just now? I saw the cutest guy."). Some narratives, though, take place in the present: ("She hails a taxi. She gets in and gives the driver the address; then she realizes she has no idea what she's going to say to Jim when she gets there.") Using the present tense can make a story feel very immediate, with urgency that past tense lacks. Very few novels are written in the future tense ("After the ball, he will go home. He will put his head in his hands and he will be sorry he didn't go up to the princess and introduce himself.") Even if the novel takes place in the future, it is usually told from the perspective of a narrator who has already lived through the events.

I Warned You!
A foreshadowed event is an event that the author suggests will happen later.

Frequently, events will be foreshadowed. *Foreshadowing* is when the author hints at something that is going to happen later. For example, a character who always forgets to lock the door might be warned by his mother that someone can easily break into the house. Later he gets robbed. That's foreshadowing (or irony, depending on whom you ask).

Plot

Telling Tales
Plot is the story.

Plot, as you may already know, is what happens in the story. It's what happens to the characters. It's what we usually answer when people ask, "What's that book about?" ("Well, it's about this boy who discovers that he can flawlessly and convincingly imitate other people's speech. He goes to school and...") Plots, when they are at their best, reveal something to the reader about the characters. It is almost always more effective and enjoyable to show something about a character through a storyline than just to tell the reader.

Genre

Both fiction and nonfiction can be categorized by genre, or type. Although you won't have to know what kind of passage you're reading, it helps to be prepared for the genres you might encounter. Some genres you might see on the test are:

Fiction

novel: a long, extended story, often incorporating smaller side plots into the main narrative

novella: a shorter version of a novel, but still longer than a short story

short story: as long as 40 pages, or as short as a paragraph

fables and parables: usually short stories

realistic fiction

historical fiction

humorous fiction

literary fiction/serious fiction: what you read in school

Nonfiction

autobiography/memoir

personal essay

academic essay

ANALYZING FICTION

In addition to the above terms, which apply to prose in general, there are a few elements that apply primarily to fiction. Just as in good poetry, where the beat and meter meld with the subject (see Chapter 8), in good fiction the elements blend together seamlessly.

Characters

Probably one of the main reasons people read is to meet new and interesting characters. Characters work in a story in many different ways. The protagonist, as you remember from the definition in the previous chapter, is the hero or heroine of the story. Most of the time, the protagonist is a sympathetic character. In other words, he or she is someone you can relate to, someone whose problems you can understand or you would want to understand. If a character is not sympathetic at all, the book may not be compelling enough to read. Think back on some of the books you have read throughout the years. How much could you sympathize with the plights of the protagonist?

Just My Type
Genre is the type of fiction or nonfiction, such as mystery, romance, and historical.

It's a Bird...
The protagonist, or the hero, is usually a sympathetic figure.

Voice

Fiction can be written in several different voices. The main ones are:

First Person

This is when the narrator is the main character in the story. It is easy to recognize because it uses the pronoun *I* in the narrative (not dialogue) part.

First-person voice is personal. Consider the first-person voice in the following passage, which immediately sets up a dialogue between the reader and the narrator. This is going to be *his* story. It is an intensely personal narrative, revealing much about the main character. It draws the reader in.

One limitation of the first-person voice is that the reader hears only one side of the story. Sometimes narrators don't tell the truth. Sometimes they don't notice everything that's happening. First-person voice is very subjective.

Drill #1

Read the following first-person passage and answer the questions that follow.

> Call me Ishmael. Some years ago—never mind
> how long precisely—having little or no money in
> my purse, I would sail about a little and see the wa-
> tery part of the world. It is a way I have of driving
> 5 off the spleen, and regulating the circulation. When-
> ever I find myself growing grim about the mouth;
> whenever it is a damp, drizzly November in my
> soul; whenever I find myself involuntarily pausing
> before coffin warehouses, and bringing up the rear
> 10 of every funeral I meet; and especially whenever my
> hypos get such an upper hand of me, that it requires
> a strong moral principle to prevent me from delib-
> erately stepping into the street, and methodically
> knocking people's hats off—then, I account it high
> 15 time to get to sea as soon as I can.
>
> (1851)

What is the effect of the use of first person?

_____

_____

_____

Where is the metaphor? What is the effect of using a metaphor?

_____

_____

_____

What is your impression of the narrator?

_____

_____

_____

All About Me
A first-person narrative uses the pronoun *I*. This voice is very personal and revealing.

Now use your answers to the questions above to answer the following questions:

1. The author's intent in this passage is most likely to

    (A) give a complete history of the character
    (B) introduce a character with humor
    (C) show the natural setting of the piece
    (D) subtly foreshadow future events
    (E) impart the character's profession

2. In line 5, the word "spleen" most nearly means

(A) path
(B) blood
(C) melancholy
(D) kidney
(E) energy

This passage is from the opening lines of one of the great classics, *Moby Dick*, by Herman Melville. Answers can be found on pages 108–109.

Third-Person

Third-person narratives use the third-person pronouns *him, her, he, she, them,* and *they.*

Third-person narration allows the author to maintain his or her own voice separate from the voices of the characters. It gives the author more freedom in that he/she is free to swoop down inside the characters' heads and tell the reader things that the characters themselves don't know. The third person can be restricted to one character's point of view, or the author may choose to show a "bird's-eye" view of the story from multiple points of view.

The third person allows for distance and objectivity. The writer is separate from the characters and can comment freely on them. He/she can remain objective and judge the characters or cast a critical eye on the proceedings. Pay attention to the interaction or relationship between the narrator/writer and the characters. Sometimes on the SAT Literature Subject Test you may be asked to identify what effect a certain word or description has on your perception of the character. You may need to identify what the author's intentions are, or if he or she is objective or subjective in tone.

Drill #2

Try the following third-person passage and answer the questions that follow.

> They had walked in single file down the path, and
> even in the open one stayed behind the other. Both
> were dressed in denim trousers and in denim coats
> with brass buttons. Both wore black, shapeless hats
> 5 and both carried tight blanket rolls slung over their
> shoulders. The first man was small and quick, dark
> of face, with restless eyes and sharp, strong features.
> Every part of him was defined: small, strong hands,
> slender arms, a thin and bony nose. Behind him
> 10 walked his opposite, a huge man, shapeless of face,
> with large, pale eyes, with wide, sloping shoulders;
> and he walked heavily, dragging his feet a little, the
> way a bear drags his paws. His arms did not swing
> at his sides, but hung loosely.
>
> (1937)

What is the effect of the third-person voice in the description?

_____

_____

_____

Is the description emotional or objective?

_____

_____

_____

Where is the metaphor, and what is the purpose of it?

_____

_____

_____

Now use your answers to the questions above to answer the following questions:

1. The structure of the passage is best described as

   (A) two characters are compared and then
       contrasted
   (B) each character is introduced and described
   (C) two characters are compared to each other and
       then each is compared to an animal
   (D) two characters' physical characteristics are
       described, followed by their clothing
   (E) characters' outward appearances are stated,
       followed by their inner thoughts

2. The tone of the passage can best be described as

   (A) barely hidden contempt
   (B) dispassionate description
   (C) unforgiving scrutiny
   (D) supernatural invention
   (E) focused inquiry

This passage is from John Steinbeck's *Of Mice and Men*. Answers can be found on page 109.

Other Points of View

You will rarely see other points of view in published works, although some recent modern novels have used them quite successfully. We mention them here in case you encounter them on future tests.

Second-Person

In second-person narration the author speaks using the pronoun "you," like a Choose-Your-Own-Adventure story ("You walk into a class. You choose the same desk you always do. You sigh wearily."). The second-person voice is often used to create a special relationship between the reader and the work. By using "you," the author in effect makes the reader a character in the book, rather than just an observer. Jay McInerney's *Bright Lights, Big City* is an example of a book written in the second person.

First-Person Plural

Another rarely used point of view is the first-person plural. This is when the narrator is a collection of first-person narrators. The book is narrated by a "we." ("We looked into the crystal ball. What we saw there scared the bejesus out of every one of us.") This technique forces the reader to concentrate more on what the story is about than on who is telling it. Jeffrey Eugenides, in his novel *The Virgin Suicides*, effectively employs this technique.

Drill #3

Now try applying what you've learned so far to the opening of this short story.

> The year was 2081, and everybody was finally
> equal. They weren't only equal before God and the
> law. They were equal every which way. Nobody was
> smarter than anybody else. Nobody was better looking
> than anybody else. Nobody was stronger or quicker
> than anybody else. All this equality was due to the
> 211th, 212th, and 213th Amendments to the Constitu-
> tion, and to the unceasing vigilance of agents of the
> U. S. Handicapper General.
> Some things about living still weren't quite right,
> though. April, for instance, still drove people crazy
> by not being springtime. And it was in that clammy
> month that the H-G men took George and Hazel
> Bergeron's fourteen-year-old son, Harrison, away.
>
> (1950)

1. The narrator's tone can best be described as

   (A) slightly satirical
   (B) harshly critical
   (C) darkly cynical
   (D) mildly emotional
   (E) excessively casual

2. The author repeats the phrase "nobody was" most likely to

   (A) introduce theme
   (B) underscore a point
   (C) instill a sense of loneliness
   (D) refute a commonly held assumption
   (E) present three contradictory elements

3. In the first paragraph, the author employs which of the following?

   (A) Internal rhymes
   (B) Mimicry of the speech of the lower class
   (C) General comparison
   (D) Parallel construction
   (E) Introduction of the protagonist

This passage is from "Harrison Bergeron," a short story in Kurt Vonnegut's collection of short stories *Welcome to the Monkey House.* Answers can be found on page 110.

ANALYZING NONFICTION

Prose writing that is not invented is called nonfiction. You have probably encountered nonfiction in the form of essay, memoir, article, biography, and autobiography. Of course, the line between fiction and nonfiction blurs when the author inserts autobiographical elements into fiction (for example, a Jewish orphan from Queens, New York writes a series of books about a Jewish orphan from Queens). And sometimes people exaggerate or distort their own experiences, so that a memoir is more like a piece of fiction.

The important thing to keep in mind when you're reading nonfiction is that you should analyze it in the same way you analyze fiction. As you read, think about the author's tone. Is the author dispassionate, ironic, satirical, or didactic (instructive)? If a thesis is provided, is the author for it, against it, or neutral? Sometimes nonfiction is objective; sometimes it is subjective. It can contain poetic language or stick to factual information and scholarly interpretation.

Nonfiction Revealed
The most familiar forms of nonfiction prose are essay, biography, and autobiography.

Drill #4

Take a look at the following passage and questions that follow.

> My name had lost its ring of familiarity and I
> had to be nudged to go and receive my diploma.
> All my preparations had fled. I neither marched up
> to the stage like a conquering Amazon, nor did I
> 5 look in the audience for Bailey's nod of approval.
> Marguerite Johnson, I heard the name again, my
> honors were read, there were noises in the audience
> of appreciation, and I took my place on the stage as
> rehearsed.
> 10   I thought about colors I hated: ecru, puce, lavender,
> beige, and black.
>
>   (1969)

1. From the passage, it is reasonable to infer that

    (A) Marguerite had never graduated before
    (B) Marguerite was surprised that her name was called
    (C) Marguerite was struck by stage fright when her name was called
    (D) Marguerite was unable to get her diploma
    (E) Marguerite was a painter

2. The sentence "I neither marched up to the stage like a conquering Amazon, nor did I look in the audience for Bailey's nod of approval" (lines 3-5) contains an example of

    (A) authorial intrusion
    (B) startling anachronism
    (C) complicated syntax
    (D) anthropomorphism
    (E) allusion

This selection is from the autobiography of Maya Angelou, *I Know Why the Caged Bird Sings*. Answers are on page 110.

Drill #5

Now put it all together with this excerpt and accompanying drill questions.

Their adobe house was the same as two decades
before, four large rooms under a thatched roof and
three square windows facing south with their frames
painted sky blue. Lin stood in the yard facing the
5   front wall while flipping over a dozen mildewed
books he had left to be sunned on a stack of fire-
wood. Sure thing, he thought, Shuyu doesn't know
how to take care of books. Maybe I should give
them to my nephews. These books are of no use to
10   me anymore.

     Beside him chickens were strutting and geese
waddling. A few little chicks were passing back
and forth through the narrow gaps in the paling
that fenced a small vegetable garden. In the garden
15   pole beans and long cucumbers hung on trellises,
eggplants curved like ox horns, and lettuce heads
were so robust that they covered up the furrows. In
addition to the poultry, his wife kept two pigs and
a goat for milk. Their sow was oinking from the
20   pigpen, which was adjacent to the western end of
the vegetable garden. Against the wall of the pigpen
a pile of manure waited to be carted to their family
plot, where it would go through high-temperature
composting in a pit for two months before being
25   put into the field. The air reeked of distillers' grains
mixed in the pig feed. Lin disliked the sour smell,
which was the only uncomfortable thing to him
here. From the kitchen, where Shuyu was cooking,
came the coughing of the bellows. In the south, elm
30   and birch crowns shaded their neighbors' straw and
titled roofs. Now and then a dog barked from one of
these homes.

     Having turned over all the books, Lin went out of
the front wall, which was three feet high and topped
35   with thorny jujube branches. In one hand he held a
dog-eared Russian dictionary he had used in high
school. Having nothing to do, he sat on their grind-
ing stone, thumbing through the old dictionary. He
still remembered some Russian vocabulary and even
40   tried to form a few short sentences in his mind with
some words. But he couldn't recall the grammati-
cal rules for the case changes exactly, so he gave up
and let the book lie on his lap. Its pages fluttered a
little as a breeze blew across. He raised his eyes to

45 watch the villagers hoeing potatoes in a distant field,
which was so vast that a red flag was planted in the
middle of it as a marker, so that they could take a
break when they reached the flag. Lin was fascinat-
ed by the sight, but he knew little about farm work.

(1999)

1. The passage as a whole can be said to be a contrast
   of

   (A) center and periphery
   (B) corruption and honesty
   (C) intellect and physicality
   (D) heaven and earth
   (E) secular and divine

2. Lin's attitude could best be described as

   (A) haughty
   (B) indifferent
   (C) inquisitive
   (D) distracted
   (E) enthralled

3. It is reasonable to infer that

   (A) Lin is a professor in the city
   (B) Lin is returning home after a long time away
   (C) Lin is on vacation
   (D) Lin is not used to the country
   (E) Lin is blind to the beauty of the country

4. Which of the following is an example of
   personification?

   (A) "Long cucumbers hung on trellises" (lines 15)
   (B) "Chickens were strutting and geese waddling"
        (lines 11-12)
   (C) "The air reeked of distillers' grains mixed in
        the pig feed (lines 25-26)
   (D) "From the kitchen, where Shuyu was cooking,
        came the coughing of the bellows" (lines 28-29)
   (E) "Their sow was oinking from the pigpen"
        (lines 19-20)

5. The lines "Sure thing, he thought, Shuyu doesn't know how to take care of books. Maybe I should give them to my nephews. These books are of no use to me anymore" (lines 7-10)

    I.   are an example of indirect dialogue
    II.   signify a shift in the narrator's focus
    III. represent a relinquishing of Lin's pastoral life

    (A) I only
    (B) II only
    (C) III only
    (D) I, II, and III
    (E) I and II

6. The "sour smell" (line 26) refers to

    (A) Shuyu's cooking
    (B) the manure near the pigpen
    (C) the pig feed
    (D) the mildewed books
    (E) the nearby field

7. The passage as a whole is best described as

    (A) a paean to rural life
    (B) an elegy for a lost time
    (C) a detailed description of a place
    (D) an epiphanic moment in a young man's life
    (E) an allegory of a homeward journey

The excerpt above is from Ha Jin's *Waiting*. Answers can be found on page 111.

Drill #6

Now test your skill on this passage.

"Try and make a clever woman of her, Lavinia; I should like her to be a clever woman."

Mrs. Penniman, at this, looked thoughtful a moment. "My dear Austin," she then inquired, "do you
5   think it is better to be clever than to be good?"

"Good for what?" asked the Doctor. "You are good for nothing unless you are clever."

From this assertion Mrs. Penniman saw no reason to dissent; she possibly reflected that her own
10 great use in the world was owing to her aptitude for many things.

"Of course I wish Catherine to be good," the Doctor said next day; "but she won't be any the less virtuous for not being a fool. I am not afraid of her
15 being wicked; she will never have the salt of malice in her character. She is 'as good as good bread,' as the French say; but six years hence I don't want to have to compare her to good bread-and-butter."

"Are you afraid she will be insipid? My dear
20 brother, it is I who supply the butter; so you needn't fear!" said Mrs. Penniman, who had taken in hand the child's "accomplishments," overlooking her at the piano, where Catherine displayed a certain talent, and going with her to the dancing-class, where
25 it must be confessed that she made but a modest figure.

Mrs. Penniman was a tall, thin, fair, rather faded woman, with a perfectly amiable disposition, a high standard of gentility, a taste for light literature, and a
30 certain foolish indirectness and obliquity of character. She was romantic; she was sentimental; she had a passion for little secrets and mysteries—a very innocent passion, for her secrets had hitherto always been as unpractical as addled eggs.

(1881)

1. The word "overlooking" (line 22) is meant to suggest that Mrs. Penniman does which of the following?

    (A) Ignores Catherine's talent
    (B) Teaches Catherine how to play the piano
    (C) Supervises Catherine's piano playing
    (D) Discourages Catherine
    (E) Hires Catherine's tutors

2. Which of the following does Mrs. Penniman use metaphorically to talk about her influence on Catherine?

   (A) Addled eggs
   (B) Butter
   (C) Bread
   (D) Salt
   (E) A fool

3. What does the author imply by the terms "it must be confessed that she made but a modest figure" (lines 25-26)?

   (A) Catherine was trim and fit.
   (B) Catherine was unaware of her talent.
   (C) Catherine was unlikely to brag.
   (D) Catherine was a talented dancer.
   (E) Catherine was just an average dancer.

4. The narrative tone in the above piece can best be described as

   (A) melodramatic
   (B) ironic
   (C) sardonic
   (D) didactic
   (E) observant

5. The narrative point of view in the above passage is that of a

   (A) third person
   (B) protagonist
   (C) second person
   (D) sarcastic first person
   (E) detached first person

6. In this context, "addled" (line 34) most nearly means

   (A) confused
   (B) useless
   (C) scrambled
   (D) burdened
   (E) rotten

This passage is from Henry James's *Washington Square*. Answers can be found on page 112.

Summary

Did you get all that?

Before you move on, make sure you understand

- o   fiction versus nonfiction
- o   tense
- o   plot
- o   genre
- o   character
- o   voice
- o   point of view

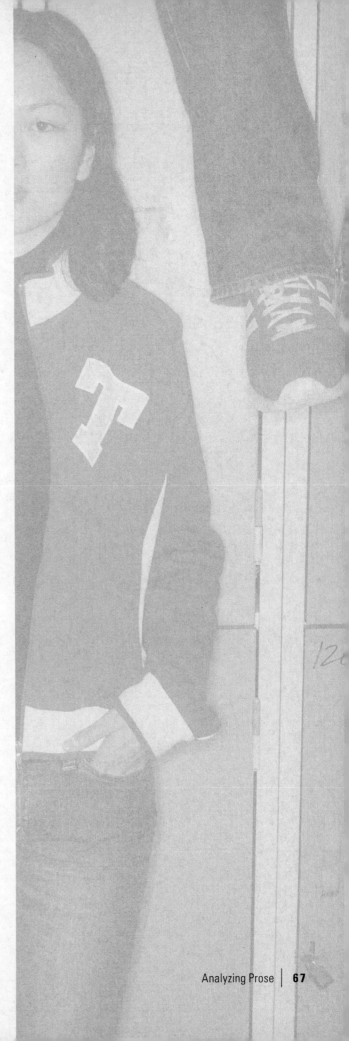

Chapter 8
Poetry Doesn't Bite

Poetry has a reputation for being unnecessarily complex and hard to understand, but often the poetry passages are the easiest ones on the SAT Literature Subject Test. In this chapter, we'll give you the tools with which you can successfully analyze poetry, including form, meter, theme, and classical and modern poetry, as well as a list of useful terms to know.

WHAT IS POETRY?

In Chapter 6 we discussed the definition of poetry: "a rhythmic expression of feelings and ideas." That's a pretty vague definition, but we keep it vague on purpose. Poetry encompasses a broad range of material. It's a category that ranges from the works of William Shakespeare to T. S. Eliot. Some people would even include the lyrics of songs as poetry, because poems are sometimes set to music.

The most useful way to approach poetry is to first be aware of the date it was written. Every poem will have the publication date at the bottom. For the purposes of the SAT Literature Subject Test, let's assume everything written before 1900 is classical, and everything written after is modern.

CLASSICAL POETRY

Classical poetry has a very formal, rigid structure. Take a look at this poem, written anonymously in 1612:

"A Pilgrim's Solace"

Stay, O sweet, and do not rise!
The light that shines comes from thine eyes;
The day breaks not: it is my heart,
Because that you and I must part.
Stay! Or else my joys will die
And perish in their infancy.

Form

Roses Are Red
A rhyme scheme is the pattern of rhyme in poetry.

This poem has a certain rhyme scheme—the scheme tells you which lines rhyme with which other lines. The rhyme scheme here is

A
A
B
B
C
C

This means the first line rhymes with the second line, the third line rhymes with the fourth line, and the fifth line rhymes with the sixth line. (In seventeenth-century speech, "die" and "infancy" rhymed.) A set of two lines in a poem (often, although not always, rhymed) is called a couplet.

You may have heard of sonnets, quatrains, epics, and other poems. For the SAT Literature Subject Test, you don't need to know them or tell them apart. Just remember that sometimes drama is written in verse (such as *Romeo and Juliet*).

Meter

Meter is the beat of the poem, like the drum beat in a song. You've probably heard of iambic pentameter (as used in Shakespeare) or anapests or tetrameter. For the SAT Literature Subject Test, you don't need to know any of this. Just be aware of how the poem sounds—if the beat is uniform and steady or if it's erratic and staccato—and then think about why that would be. A regular meter sounds soothing, like a pop song, whereas unmetered poetry can sound harsh or surprising.

Whenever you see an "ancient" date, a rhyme scheme, or a specific meter, you can bet you're dealing with classical poetry. Or if a modern poet has chosen to use these devices, it's probably to convey a sense of tradition or traditional themes.

Theme

Imagine reading a Shakespearean sonnet that was about urban crime or teenage drug use. Check the expiration date on your milk if this happens—something is wrong. Urban crime and teenage drug use were not the hot topics of pre–twentieth century poetry. Classical poetry dealt with classical themes: love, love lost, beauty, death, or nature. Metaphors pretty much compare plants, animals, or situations to lovers, death, or truth (and all of truth's subsections: loyalty, betrayal, yearning, unrequited love . . . you know, BIG THOUGHTS).

Classical themes are universal and general. A love poem often is more about love than it is about a lover. Also, on the SAT Literature Subject Test, most classical love poems are more about the one who loves and his feelings, emotions, and suffering than about the beloved. The poems could have been written to any Thomasina, Dika, or Harmonia on the block. Seldom are there any specifics about how the object of affection looks, acts, or feels, or who she is or what she says.

Beat It
Meter = The beat of the poem.

Drill #1

Try out some questions about the anonymous poem you looked at earlier.

"A Pilgrim's Solace"

Stay, O sweet, and do not rise!
The light that shines comes from thine eyes;
The day breaks not: it is my heart,
Because that you and I must part.
Stay! Or else my joys will die
And perish in their infancy.

What is this poem about?
a beloved leaving a lover

Who is the narrator of this poem?
a man

What do we know about the narrator?
he is in love

What do we know about the beloved in this poem?
she is leaving him

Is there a pattern of rhyme and meter?
yes

Now use this information to answer these questions.

1. Which of the following can be found in the poem?

   (A) Onomatopoeia
   (B) Ascertainable rhyme scheme
   (C) Oxymoron
   (D) Change in perspective
   (E) Unsolved paradox

2. Which of the following can be inferred from the poem?

   (A) It is not really morning.
   (B) There will be trouble if she is found in his room.
   (C) The woman will follow his wishes.
   (D) They are both in bed.
   (E) She makes him happy.

Answers can be found on page 113.

MODERN TIMES

Just as music grew from formal sonatas and fugues to rock 'n roll and jazz fusion, so poetry has evolved from sonnets and other restrictive forms into free and blank verse.

> **FREE VERSE** is a poem without regular meter or line length.
>
> **BLANK VERSE** is an unrhymed poem with a regular meter.

Free and blank verse are favorite forms for modern poets. Generally, the best way to decide if a poem is metered is to count the syllables. If the poem has a regular beat, then it's blank verse. Most modern poems are written in free verse, however.

Land of the Free
Modern poetry tends to use free or blank verse.

It's wise to use what you know about a poet or a poem when you analyze modern poetry. Modern poetry is much more likely to be about social issues or current events than classical poetry is, although modern poetry can still tackle love and beauty. Like death and taxes, love and beauty are always with us—hence, the popularity of soap operas.

Take a look at the date the poem was written. Was it written after World War I (1914–1918), when people were shocked by the brutality of modern warfare? Around World War II, when pure evil raised its ugly head (1939–1945)? Just after the war, when most English language writers were exuberant and flushed with victory? After 1950, when mass production and television began to burrow their way into U.S. homes? During the Civil Rights movement of the 1960s and 1970s, when issues of racial equality and women's liberation were foremost in the public's thoughts? More recently, when environmentalism gained importance?

How Old Are You Now?
The poem's date can sometimes help you determine its theme.

Also, take a look at the language the poem uses—its diction. Does it sound like someone speaking? If so, who does it sound like? Without resorting to stereotyping, does it sound like someone from the South in the United States? A British person? An African American? Is the language stilted and formal or flowing and full of slang?

What'd You Say?
Diction is the language an author uses, his or her word choice.

Which issues would be important to the narrator of the poem? What's the imagery the poet uses? Modern cities or ghettos? The countryside? A farmer might lament the loss of his land or how his way of life is slowly eroding, but he probably won't care too much about the plight of the inner-city immigrant. Similarly, war refugees landing in the United States probably don't worry too much about nature. In other words, city poems generally won't use nature images, and pastoral poems won't use urban, industrial images.

He's Got Issues
Think about the issues that might be important to the poem's narrator.

All that being said, the point of departing from strict form and meter is to free the poet from convention. So the poem doesn't have to follow the rules we just explained. The above are just some general guidelines. If you read a poem that seems to defy the universal principles discussed here, then perhaps it's just a poet stretching his or her wings, so to speak (metaphor alert!). Don't worry about it, and go with your gut.

POETRAPHOBIA AND OTHER CURABLE DISEASES

People tend to fear poetry, which is completely unnecessary considering that there are real things to worry about, such as spiders and werewolves. Although it's true that poetry can be somewhat daunting because it is not necessarily as clear as prose, it's often easier to decipher a poem than it is to decipher a really complex sentence.

Poems are generally shorter than fiction. That means less reading and more time for analysis. This is good, considering that the SAT Literature Subject Test is only one hour long. In addition, the entire poem is reprinted on the page. So there's no confusing backstory that you need to know (as you might for a novel excerpt). Usually, there is just one overarching theme, in contrast to the many themes you'll find in a novel. And it's easier to break down a poem into its distinct parts. Often, each line is a new thought, idea, or image, so it's easy to find specific references within a poem.

> ## Poetry Versus Prose
> Reasons that poetry is often easier to interpret than prose:
>
> - Poems are generally shorter
> - Usually, the entire poem is printed on the page
> - Often poems have just one theme or idea
> - Poems are easier to break down into distinct parts

The mistake most people make when approaching a poem is trying to read the whole thing before answering the questions. Poetry can be a tough nut to crack (another metaphor alert!) because it's pretty dense, so it assaults you with a bunch of images, which, taken individually, can help you form a picture of what the entire poem is about.

Drill #2

Let's take a look at some modern poetry.

"Brass Spittoons"

Clean the spittoons, boy.
Detroit,
Chicago,
Atlantic City,
5   Palm Beach.
Clean the spittoons.
The steam in hotel kitchens,
And the smoke in hotel lobbies,
And the slime in hotel spittoons:
10 Part of my life.

Hey, boy!
A nickel,
A dime,
A dollar,
15 Two dollars a day.
Hey, boy!
A nickel,
A dime,
A dollar,
20 Two dollars
Buys shoes for the baby.
House rent to pay.
God on Sunday.
My God!

25 Babies and church
and women and Sunday
all mixed up with dimes and
dollars and clean spittoons
and house rent to pay.
30 Hey, boy!

A bright bowl of brass is beautiful to the Lord.
Bright polished brass like the cymbals
Of King David's dancers,
Like the wine cups of Solomon.
35 Hey, boy!
A clean spittoon on the altar of the Lord.
A clean bright spittoon all newly polished,—
At least I can offer that.
Com'mere boy!

(1927)

So what do you notice right off the bat? Well, there are names of cities. (Urban themes!) There is steam, smoke, and slime. (Dirty cities!) Someone is calling a boy. (Power!) Money is changing hands. (Commerce!) Then there's all this religious stuff. (Lofty themes! BIG THOUGHTS!)

See? We already know a little bit about what the poem is about. But let's look closer. See if you can find some of the literary techniques you learned about in Chapter 6. Make sure you write down the answers in the space provided.

What are some examples of alliteration?

_____

_____

_____

Which words are repeated? Why do you think the author does this?

_____

_____

_____

Where does the author use allusion?

_____

_____

_____

Now let's try some specific questions about the poem.

1. In line 31, "a bright bowl of brass is beautiful to the Lord," the author is most likely

    (A) making an analogy
    (B) describing a glorious church scene
    (C) using alliteration to emphasize a point
    (D) comparing the bowls to the cymbals on the following line
    (E) suggesting that poetry is like prayer

2. The list of cities in lines 2-5 implies

    (A) the narrator is educated in geography
    (B) the narrator is reading a newspaper
    (C) the poem could be occurring in any of these cities
    (D) the poem is an extended analogy
    (E) the cities are symbols of oppressed people

3. In lines 20-21, "Two dollars buys shoes for the baby" is an example of

   (A) personification
   (B) haphazard alliteration
   (C) repetition of a phrase
   (D) economic calculation
   (E) illustrative allusion

4. The narrator of the poem is most likely

   (A) in charge of the hotel maids and janitors
   (B) generous with his tips
   (C) proud of his work
   (D) an outspoken critic
   (E) a stingy father

How did that go? Now we know even more about the poem, and we're ready to answer some general questions.

5. The narrator is best characterized as

   (A) honest and reverent
   (B) selfish and complaining
   (C) ignorant and obliging
   (D) hard-working and dutiful
   (E) religious and childlike

6. Which of the following best describes the nature of the poem in its entirety?

   (A) A realistic pastoral scene
   (B) An eloquent description of a place
   (C) A religious allegory
   (D) A didactic narrative
   (E) An impassioned portrait

7. The rhythm of the poem adds to the poem's theme in which of the following ways?

   I.   It mimics the actions of the speaker.
   II. It contrasts the secular with the divine.
   III. It adds to the lyricism of the poem.

   (A) I only
   (B) II only
   (C) III only
   (D) I and II only
   (E) I, II, and III

8. The last three lines emphasize which of the following?

   (A) The hopelessness of the speaker's situation
   (B) The emptiness of the speaker's job
   (C) The fragility of the speaker's faith
   (D) The speaker's perseverance
   (E) The comfort the speaker finds in his spirituality

It's Not What It Seems
Although this looks like a line-reference question, it's asking about the function of a word repeated throughout the poem—a general question about theme.

9. The lines "Hey, Boy!" (11, 16, 30, 35) are most likely

   (A) the speaker calling his son
   (B) a derogatory command
   (C) an impolite greeting
   (D) an urban colloquialism
   (E) the speaker's conscience

10. The poem suggests that

   (A) poverty is arduous
   (B) thriftiness is a virtue
   (C) brass is a relatively recently discovered metal
   (D) imagination offers escape
   (E) good things come to those who wait

By the way, "Brass Spittoons" was written by Langston Hughes, one of the most prominent figures of the Harlem Renaissance. Answers can be found on pages 113–114.

Drill #3

Now try the techniques on this poem.

> "There Is No Frigate Like a Book"
>
> There is no frigate like a book
>   To take us lands away,
> Nor any coursers like a page
>   Of prancing poetry.
> 5 This traverse may the poorest take
>   Without oppress of toll;
> How frugal is the chariot
>   That bears a human soul!
>
>   (c. 1890)

What are the examples of similes?

_____

_____

_____

What are the examples of metaphors?

_____

_____

_____

What is an example of personification?

_____

_____

_____

Is there rhythm and meter? Describe.

_____

_____

_____

What do you think is the main idea of the poem?

_____

_____

_____

Be More Specific
Don't forget to do specific
questions first.

1. The poem implies

    (A) boats are unlike books
    (B) it is better to have a vehicle for the body than for the mind
    (C) there are more books than boats
    (D) books are excellent ways to experience the world
    (E) the author values the practical over the frivolous

2. In line 3, "coursers" most nearly means

    (A) swift horses
    (B) slow skiffs
    (C) textbooks
    (D) ancient chariots
    (E) poetic devices

3. The diction of the poem is characterized by

    (A) an abundance of description
    (B) lofty syntax
    (C) forceful actions
    (D) humorous word play
    (E) awkward contrasts

4. Which of the following does the poem imply?

    (A) The poor are less likely to travel than the rich.
    (B) Saved money should be put toward travel.
    (C) Literature is an inexpensive means of escape.
    (D) Literature should be free.
    (E) Literature can touch a person's soul.

5. It is reasonable to infer that

    (A) the speaker prefers action to passivity
    (B) the speaker thinks there is great power in the written word
    (C) the speaker enjoys travel narratives
    (D) the speaker has an active fantasy life
    (E) the speaker values frugality as a virtue

6. In line 5, "This traverse" refers metaphorically to

    (A) the journey across the river of life
    (B) the path toward wisdom
    (C) getting lost in a book
    (D) the process of education
    (E) the inevitability of old age

7. The speaker's tone is best described as

   (A) cheerfully lecturing
   (B) forcefully instructive
   (C) tirelessly proactive
   (D) gently persuasive
   (E) selfishly sincere

"There Is No Frigate Like a Book" was written by Emily Dickinson (1830–1886). Her simple poems are filled with imagery. Answers can be found on pages 115–116.

Drill #4

Now try the techniques out on this next poem. Instead of writing down answers to questions, think about alliteration, rhythm, personification, theme, etc., while you're reading. Don't forget to do the specific questions first.

"The Dying Christian to His Soul"

Vital spark of heav'nly flame!
Quit, O quit this mortal frame:
Trembling, hoping, ling'ring, flying,
O the pain, the bliss of dying!
5 Cease, fond Nature, cease thy strife,
And let me languish into life.

Hark! they whisper; angels say,
Sister Spirit, come away!
What is this absorbs me quite?
10 Steals my senses, shuts my sight,
Drowns my spirits, draws my breath?
Tell me, my soul, can this be death?

The world recedes; it disappears!
Heav'n opens on my eyes! my ears
15 With sounds seraphic ring!
Lend, lend your wings! I mount! I fly!
O Grave! where is thy victory?
O Death! where is thy sting?

(c. 1712)

1. The author of the poem uses all of the following EXCEPT

    (A) expressive punctuation
    (B) a particular rhyme scheme
    (C) regular meter
    (D) adjectives
    (E) Biblical allusion

2. The question "O Death! where is thy sting?" can best be described as

    (A) harshly rhetorical
    (B) dubiously questioning
    (C) gently taunting
    (D) gravely earnest
    (E) paradoxical

3. Which of the following is NOT an active verb?

   (A) "Quit" (line 2)
   (B) "Draws" (line 11)
   (C) "Tell" (line 12)
   (D) "Sounds" (line 15)
   (E) "Ring" (line 15)

4. The three stanzas differ in that

   (A) the first addresses nature, the second
       addresses the soul, and the third addresses
       angels
   (B) the first speaks of dying, the second speaks of
       the loss of sense, and the third speaks of life
       after death
   (C) the first stanza describes death as purely
       painful, the second describes the loss of
       sense, and the third describes angels
   (D) the speaker of the first stanza is mortal, the
       speaker of the second is angelic, and the
       speaker of the third is death
   (E) the first stanza welcomes death, the second
       stanza taunts it, and the third stanza
       reluctantly accepts it

5. By "frame" (line 2), the author most likely means

   (A) a picture of the world
   (B) a previously held image of death
   (C) a cage for the soul
   (D) a metaphorical skeleton
   (E) the mortal body

6. The overall theme of the poem is best stated as

   (A) death is sublime even though it is painful
   (B) death is the victory of heaven over the soul
   (C) death can be resisted but it always eventually
       wins
   (D) even if one suffers in this life, the next life will
       be better
   (E) pain is only temporary; death is eternal

7. The style of the poem can best be described as

   (A) ornately romantic
   (B) playfully suggestive
   (C) harshly critical
   (D) elaborately descriptive
   (E) emotionally cryptic

8. The questions in the last two lines serve mostly to emphasize

   (A) the speaker's surprise at how little death hurts
   (B) the mental ecstasy of death overshadowing physical pain
   (C) the battle that is fought between the body and the soul
   (D) the speaker's antagonistic relationship with death
   (E) the transient nature of death

FYI, the poem is by Alexander Pope, who lived from 1688–1744. Answers can be found on pages 116–117.

Drill #5

Let's try a more recent poem.

"Madman's Song"

Better to see your cheek grown hollow,
Better to see your temple worn,
Than to forget to follow, follow,
After the sound of a silver horn.

5   Better to bind your brow with willow
And follow, follow until you die,
Than to sleep with your head on a golden pillow,
Nor lift it up when the hunt goes by.

Better to see your cheek grown sallow
10 And your hair grown gray, so soon, so soon,
Than to forget to hallo, hallo,
After the milk-white hounds of the moon.

(c. 1921)

1. What is the effect of using "silver" to describe the "horn" (line 4)?

   (A) To imply that the horn is not as valuable as a golden horn
   (B) To foreshadow any item that may be used in the "hunt" (line 8)
   (C) To be alliterative with the word "sound"
   (D) To indicate that the image would be bright
   (E) To symbolize the beauty of wealth

2. Given in context, the word "hallo" (line 11) is probably meant to convey which of the following?

   (A) A form of greeting
   (B) Another form of the word "hollow" (line 1)
   (C) An echo
   (D) A sound that hounds might make such as baying at the moon
   (E) A variation on the word "halo"

3. The attitude of the author toward the reader is best described as

   (A) openly hostile
   (B) gently insistent
   (C) didactic
   (D) ambivalent
   (E) disgusted

4. The author is most probably addressing the poem to someone

   (A) who has lost touch with what is important
   (B) who is ashamed of her background
   (C) who has become very wealthy
   (D) who is about to die
   (E) who is vain

5. In this poem, the images are meant to convey which of the following?

   I. Someone who has been committed to an insane asylum
   II. Someone who has lost passion for life
   III. Someone who has been filled with passion

   (A) I only
   (B) II only
   (C) II and III only
   (D) III only
   (E) I, II, and III

6. The repetition in the poem most likely

   (A) helps the rhyme scheme
   (B) emphasizes the main theme
   (C) chastises the reader
   (D) reveals the speaker's anger
   (E) contrasts the laziness of the person addressed

By the way, "Madman's Song" was written by William Rose Benét in 1921. Answers can be found on page 117.

Summary

Did you get all that?

Make sure you remember the following before moving on:

- Rhyme scheme is the rhythm of rhyme.

- Meter is the beat to a poem—the syllable count.

- Identifying a poem's theme is often the key to answering general questions.

- Modern poetry often breaks free of classical restraints and conventions.

- There's no need to fear poetry!

Chapter 9
Drama Queens (and Kings and Princes and the Occasional Duchess)

Although drama appears very seldom on the SAT Literature Subject Test, we do want you to be prepared in case it rears its head. In this chapter, we list some drama terms you should know, and give you strategies to approach this specific genre.

WHAT IS DRAMA?

Drama is a form of literature unlike any other in the sense that it is not supposed to remain on the page. It is intended to be acted out. So it is always a tad strange to be reading a play silently to yourself, when it begs to be imbued with life and speech.

The elements of drama are similar to the elements of prose and poetry. There are characters, plot(s), and theme(s). Plays tend to be a bit heavier on story than other forms of literature because, well, they're about people doing things, more than they're about people thinking. Plays can also be more overtly political than other forms of literature because they have to reveal something about the characters' surroundings and interactions. They therefore lend themselves to social commentary.

Remember as you read that plays were the original movies and television programs. In times before most people could read or have access to books, plays were the main form of entertainment and instruction to the masses. Try to picture someone on stage saying the lines as you read them.

When analyzing a play, ask yourself the same questions you would if you were analyzing prose or poetry. (Don't forget that classical drama is sometimes written in verse.) If literary devices such as metaphors or similes are used, what are their effects? What is the character's tone? Are the characters archetypes (perfect examples of a type of character)? Are they designed to represent something other than what they appear to be?

In a play, the characters are central to advancing and explaining the plot. There is no outside description of what the characters say. So plays are, obviously, mostly dialogue, a fact that presents special challenges to playwrights.

Because plays generally lack narration, playwrights have improvised devices to get narrative points across. In Thornton Wilder's *Our Town,* that favorite of high school drama programs, the stage manager wanders on and off the stage commenting on the action, giving the audience his own personal insight. Other playwrights allow the characters to speak directly to the audience. Still others try to control exactly how the actors will act, by giving them detailed instructions about tone, placement, and gesture.

Since drama makes up only 10 percent of the test, there will be at most one passage of drama on your exam. Don't be surprised if it doesn't appear at all. Recently, most of the drama on the SAT Literature Subject Test has been culled from other cultures, for example, Australian or South African drama.

Although most drama is written as prose, early classical drama was written in verse. If you're analyzing drama that is written in verse, use the same techniques that you would use to analyze poetry.

A Little Drama…
Drama makes up 0–20 percent of the test. You'll see one passage at most, and many tests don't have any drama at all!

Want Drama?
Some drama is written in prose, and some drama is written in verse.

DRAMA TERMS

ASIDE: The device through which the character addresses the audience directly. The other characters cannot hear him, and the play seems to "freeze" while the character speaks. Shakespeare was fond of this device.

COMEDY: A play that is primarily for amusement or meant to provoke laughter.

FARCE: Satire bordering on the silly or ridiculous.

GENRE: The type or category of a play, such as tragedy, comedy, farce, or surrealism/theater of the absurd.

MONOLOGUE: A long passage during which only one person talks.

SOLILOQUY: A speech addressed to the audience where one character expounds upon his predicament.

STAGE DIRECTIONS: Authorial instructions inserted in parentheses to tell the actor/director how to act, move, or speak. (Stage directions can be fragments of sentences and are usually written in present tense.)

> Example: ANNA (*briskly*): Well, we can't be having any more of that. (*She stands next to Burt.*)

SURREALISM/THEATER OF THE ABSURD: This is more of a style than a form. Absurd plays often don't have a logical progression of narrative or a clear sequence of events or theme. Samuel Beckett is considered the English language master of surrealist or absurdist theater (*Waiting for Godot*). Most likely, this will not appear on the SAT Literature Subject Test.

TRAGEDY: A play that is sad or addresses sorrowful or difficult themes.

FORM

Just as you can tell the difference visually between poetry and prose, so too does drama wear different clothing (personification alert!). The speaker is identified by a new line, his or her name rendered in capital letters followed by a colon. Whenever the speaker changes, his or her name will begin on the next line.

Example:

> MOTHER: Joanne, why are you wearing that dress?

> JOANNE: Because Aunt Sally gave it to me before she died.

Drill #1

Try some of the techniques you learned in the chapters on poetry and prose to complete this drama exercise. Do the specific questions first and the general ones next.

> ELIZA (*overwhelmed*): Ah-ah-ow-oo!
>
> HIGGINS: There! That's all you'll get out of Eliza. Ah-ah-ow-oo! No use explaining. As a military man you ought to know that. Give her orders: that's what she wants. Eliza: you are to live here for the next six months, learning how to speak beautifully, like a lady in a florist's shop. If you're good and do whatever you're told, you shall sleep in a proper bedroom, and have lots to eat, and money to buy chocolates and take rides in taxis. If you're naughty and idle, you will sleep in the back kitchen among the black beetles, and be walloped by Mrs. Pearce with a broomstick. At the end of six months you shall go to Buckingham Palace in a carriage, beautifully dressed. If the King finds out you're not a lady, you will be taken to the Tower of London, where your head will be cut off as a warning to other presumptuous flower girls. If you are not found out, you shall have a present of seven and six pence to start life with as a lady in a shop. If you refuse this offer you will be a most ungrateful and wicked girl, and the angels will weep for you.
>
> (1916)

Remember:
Don't forget to circle EXCEPT and mark a Y or an N next to each answer choice.

1. The central contrasts in the passage are expressed in all of the following pairs EXCEPT

   (A) "A lady in a florist's shop" ... "flower girls"
   (B) "Buckingham Palace" ... "the Tower of London"
   (C) "Mrs. Pearce" ... "the King"
   (D) "proper bedroom" ... "the back kitchen"
   (E) "good and do whatever you're told" ... "naughty and idle"

2. From his speech, it seems clear that Higgins views Eliza as

   (A) a willful child
   (B) an obedient servant
   (C) a potential wife
   (D) a futile project
   (E) a witless pawn

3. According to the passage, all of the following are characteristic of a "lady" EXCEPT

   (A) articulate speech
   (B) employment in a florist's shop
   (C) private transportation
   (D) fine clothing
   (E) the leisure not to work

4. The amount of dialogue given to each character illustrates

   (A) the essential inequality of the two characters
   (B) the difference in the two characters' means of expression
   (C) the extent of Higgins's prejudice
   (D) Higgins's opinion of Eliza's abilities
   (E) Eliza's inability to follow Higgins's instructions

5. Higgins's speech can best be described as

   (A) condescending
   (B) didactic
   (C) instructive
   (D) explicatory
   (E) persuasive

6. It can be inferred from the passage that Eliza feels

   (A) insecure
   (B) bombarded
   (C) confused
   (D) ineffectual
   (E) insignificant

This excerpt is from *Pygmalion*, by Bernard Shaw. Answers can be found on pages 118.

Drill #2

SIR EDWARD TRENCHARD: Good morning, Coyle, good morning. (*With affected ease.*) There is a chair, Coyle. (*They sit.*) So you see those infernal tradespeople are pretty troublesome.

5 COYLE: My agent's letter this morning announces that Walter and Brass have got judgment and execution on their amount for repairing your town house last season. (*Refers to papers.*) Boquet and Barker announce their intention of taking this same course with the wine account.

10 Handmarth is preparing for a settlement of his heavy demand for the stables. Then there is Temper for pictures and other things and Miss Florence Trenchard's account with Madame Pompon, and—

SIR EDWARD: Confound it, why harass me with details,
15 these infernal particulars? Have you made out the total?

COYLE: Four thousand, eight hundred and thirty pounds, nine shillings and sixpence.

SIR EDWARD: Well, of course we must find means of settling this extortion.

20 COYLE: Yes, Sir Edward, if possible.

SIR EDWARD: If possible?

COYLE: I, as your agent, must stoop to detail, you must allow me to repeat, if possible.

SIR EDWARD: Why, you don't say there will be any dif-
25 ficulty in raising the money?

COYLE: What means would you suggest, Sir Edward?

SIR EDWARD: That, sir, is your business.

COYLE: A foretaste in the interest on the Fanhille & El-lenthrope mortgages, you are aware both are in the arrears,
30 the mortgagees in fact, write here to announce their inten-tions to foreclose. (*Shows papers.*)

SIR EDWARD: Curse your impudence, pay them off.

COYLE: How, Sir Edward?

SIR EDWARD: Confound it, sir, which of us is the agent?
35 Am I to find you brains for your own business?

COYLE: No, Sir Edward, I can furnish the brains, but what I ask of you is to furnish the money.

SIR EDWARD: There must be money somewhere, I came into possession of one of the finest properties in Hamp-
40 shire only twenty-six years ago, and now you mean to tell me I cannot raise 4,000 pounds?

COYLE: The fact is distressing, Sir Edward, but so it is.

SIR EDWARD: There's the Ravensdale property unencumbered.

45 COYLE: There, Sir Edward, you are under a mistake. The Ravensdale property is deeply encumbered, to nearly its full value.

SIR EDWARD (*Springing up.*): Good heavens.

COYLE: I have found among my father's papers a mort-
50 gage of that very property to him.

SIR EDWARD: To your father! My father's agent? Sir, do you know that if this be true I am something like a beggar, and your father something like a thief.

COYLE: I see the first plainly, Sir Edward, but not the
55 second.

SIR EDWARD: Do you forget, sir, that your father was a charity boy, fed, clothed by my father?

COYLE: Well, Sir Edward?

SIR EDWARD: And do you mean to tell me, sir, that your
60 father repaid that kindness by robbing his benefactor?

COYLE: Certainly not, but by advancing money to that benefactor when he wanted it, and by taking the security of one of his benefactor's estates, as any prudent man would under the circumstances.

65 SIR EDWARD: Why, then, sir, the benefactor's property is yours.

COYLE: I see one means, at least, of keeping the Ravensdale estate in the family.

SIR EDWARD: What is it?

70 COYLE: By marrying your daughter to the mortgagee.

SIR EDWARD: To you?

COYLE: I am prepared to settle the estate on Miss Trenchard the day she becomes Mrs. Richard Coyle.

SIR EDWARD (*Springing up.*): You insolent scoundrel,
75 how dare you insult me in my own house, sir. Leave it, sir, or I will have you kicked out by my servants.

COYLE: I never take an angry man at his word, Sir Edward. Give a few moments reflection to my offer, you can have me kicked out afterwards.

80 SIR EDWARD: (*Pacing stage.*): A beggar, Sir Edward Trenchard a beggar, see my children reduced to labor for their bread, to misery perhaps; but the alternative, Florence detests him, still the match would save her, at least,

from ruin. He might take the family name, I might re-
85 trench, retire, to the continent for a few years. Florence's
health might serve as a pretence. Repugnant as the alternative is, yet it deserves consideration.

COYLE: (*Who has watched.*): Now, Sir Edward, shall I
ring for the servants to kick me out?

1. The phrase "judgment and execution" most likely
   means

   (A) a sentence and the death penalty
   (B) the moral high ground
   (C) an official breakup of a partnership
   (D) a judge's decision and a court order
   (E) a search and seizure of property

2. Coyle and Sir Edward's relationship is that of

   (A) money manager and client
   (B) lawyer and defendant
   (C) servant and master
   (D) benefactor and recipient
   (E) uncle and nephew

3. The word "security" (line 62) most nearly means

   (A) collateral
   (B) agreement
   (C) assurance
   (D) welfare
   (E) prize

4. Which of Sir Edward's choice of words makes it
   clear that he considers the bills from his creditors
   to be unfair?

   (A) "infernal" (line 15)
   (B) "confound" (line 14)
   (C) "extortion" (line 19)
   (D) "impudence" (line 32)
   (E) "unencumbered" (lines 43-44)

5. What is the deal Coyle wants to strike with Sir Edward?

    (A) He will pay off the creditors in exchange for allowing him to marry Sir Edward's daughter.

    (B) He will give Ravensdale back to Sir Edward in exchange for allowing him to marry Sir Edward's daughter.

    (C) He will arrange the marriage of Sir Edward's daughter to the current residents of Ravensdale.

    (D) He will marry Sir Edward's daughter to prevent her at least from financial ruin.

    (E) Because Sir Edward is without money, Sir Edward will have to sanction the love affair between Coyle and his daughter.

6. Sir Edward's final lines, "A beggar, Sir Edward Trenchard a beggar, see my children reduced to labor for their bread, to misery perhaps; but the alternative, Florence detests him, still the match would save her, at least, from ruin. He might take the family name, I might retrench, retire, to the continent for a few years. Florence's health might serve as a pretence. Repugnant as the alternative is, yet it deserves consideration" (lines 80-87), are an example of

    (A) a monologue expressing doubt

    (B) a character dissolving into madness

    (C) a character addressing the audience

    (D) a character voicing both sides of an argument to himself

    (E) a speech explaining a plot point to the audience

FYI, this is from *An Enemy of the People,* by Henrik Ibsen. Answers can be found on page 119.

Summary

Did you get all that?

Make sure you can define the following terms:

- aside
- comedy
- farce
- form
- genre
- monologue
- soliloquy
- stage directions
- surrealism
- tragedy

Chapter 10
Final Thoughts

You're almost ready for the big day! Now here are some tips for the day of the test and some things you should be SURE to remember. Also, we included a complete list of all the terms we mentioned in this book, to make it easier for you to study them.

FINAL THOUGHTS

You've already covered quite a lot of information in reading about the ways to analyze poetry, prose, and drama. Before you take a practice test, do a quick review of the previous chapters, concentrating on information you might have missed or forgotten since you first read it. After taking the practice tests, review your performance, and see where your study time can best be spent. Don't waste a lot of time on one or two little things that you've missed. Rather, look for the bigger trends.

Also, review the scoring chart (Chapter 4) before your exam. Keep track of your goals. Write them down. Often, you don't need to get that many more questions right to get a really great score.

THINGS TO REMEMBER

- Put the passages in order before you begin. Which one will you do first? Last? Feel free to write numbers on the test booklet.
- If you skip questions, make sure you circle or star the number to make it very obvious that you need to go back to that question.
- Tackle specific/line-reference questions first. Read a few lines before and after for context.
- Do general questions next.
- Save weird questions for the end.
- Put answers in your own words before you go back to the answer choices.
- Pick a bubbling method, and adhere to it like glue (simile alert!).
- Slow down!

A Word on Vocabulary

Although the SAT Literature Subject Test does not necessarily test vocabulary, if you don't know the words in the answer choices, it's hard to answer the questions. As you take these tests, and as you read in general (books, newspapers, magazines, etc.), keep a list of vocabulary words that pertain to the SAT Literature Subject Test. Adjectives will be especially useful for this test; words that describe tone or attitude will also help. Make flash cards of your lists, and memorize these words. Even if they don't appear on the test, they're useful for the SAT, and they'll also impress your freshman English professor in college.

Great Literature

As you read, whether for pleasure or for school assignments, keep in mind the techniques we've discussed. While you're in the middle of the book, stop and think about tone, theme, literary devices, etc. It will help you do well on the test and on any essays you might have to write in the future.

Obviously, reading *An American Tragedy* will help more than the latest unauthorized celebrity bio, but even mind candy has themes.

SOME THINGS TO DO BEFORE THE TEST

Register early for the test. Make sure you know exactly where the test site is and how you're getting there. Don't forget, the test is administered on the weekend, when public transportation and traffic patterns might be different from your weekday routine.

Plan to reward yourself. You've worked really hard, and you deserve a little reward, whether it's a night out with your friends or that new CD you've been coveting. You might ask a parent to cook your favorite food for dinner. Or you may want to go see the latest Jackie Chan flick. Whatever. In other words, plan something for after the test so that when you are midway through the test and contemplating trading in your college plans for a career as a summer lifeguard (anything to get out of the test), you can remember your reward and make it through the next half hour.

What'll be your reward? Write it down.

The Day of the Test

On the morning of the test, set multiple alarms. Eat a little breakfast, even if you're not normally a morning muncher (toast will do). Follow your normal morning routine—for example, if you usually have coffee, have coffee. If you're not a coffee drinker, stay away from it. Organize the things you need into a pile the night before.

Don't Forget

- a plethora of No. 2 pencils with high-quality erasers
- a reliable watch
- some light reading, such as a magazine or book, to occupy your mind in case you have to wait
- a small snack, such as a granola bar or an energy bar, just in case
- a bottle of water
- layers of comfortable clothing (the test site may be hot or cold, so wear a T-shirt and bring long sleeves, just in case)
- a hair tie if you have long hair
- tissues if you have a cold or allergies
- your glasses, if you wear them (duh!)

Visit the restroom before the test starts. Try to leave anything of value at home, especially if you're unfamiliar with the test site. Different test sites have different rules and accommodations for your personal belongings, and you don't want to be worried about your MP3 player out there in the hallway when you should be thinking about metaphors.

Relax. You'll do great!

After the Test

Stretch, breathe a big sigh of relief, refuse to talk about how you did, and . . . enjoy your reward! Your score should be posted online in about two weeks. Because you've prepared yourself well for the SAT Literature Subject Test, you can wait with supreme confidence for your well-deserved scores. Have fun at the college of your choice!

REVIEW OF TERMS

allegory   a story with underlying symbols that really represent something else

alliteration   the use of a repeated consonant sound, usually at the beginning of a series of words

allusion   a reference to something or someone, usually literary

anachronism   the placement of a person or object in an inappropriate historical situation

analogy   a comparison of something to something else

anecdote   a short narrative, story, or tale

antagonist   the major character opposing the protagonist

anthropomorphism   the assignment of human attributes, such as emotions or physical characteristics, to nonhuman things

aside   a device through which the character addresses the audience directly

blank verse   an unrhymed poem with a regular meter

character   a person in a drama or novel

comedy   a play that is primarily for amusement or meant to provide laughter

diction   the author's choice of words

fable   a story that has a moral, usually involving animals as the main characters

farce   a satire that's bordering on the silly or ridiculous

figurative language   language characterized by figures of speech, such as metaphors and similes, as well as elaborate expression through imagery

form   the rhyme scheme of a poem

free verse   a poem without regular meter or line length

genre   a type, or category, of fiction or nonfiction

hyperbole   a deliberate exaggeration

irony   an expression of meaning that is the opposite of the literal meaning

metaphor   a comparison that does not use the words "like" or "as"

meter   the rhythm of a poem

monologue   a long passage during which only one person talks

narrative   a literary representation of an event or story—the text itself

onomatopoeia   a word intended to simulate the actual sound of the thing or action it describes

oxymoron   a phrase in which the words are contradictory

parable   a story that has a moral

paradox   a phrase that appears to be contradictory but which actually contains some basic truth that resolved the apparent contradiction

parallelism   the repetition of sounds, meanings, or structures to create a certain style

parody   a literary work in which the style of an author is imitated for comic effect or ridicule

pastoral   a work that deals with the lives of people, especially shepherds, in the country or in nature (as opposed to people in the city)

pathos   something that evokes a feeling of pity or sympathy

personification   the assignment of human attributes to something nonhuman

perspective   the place from which the narrator or character sees things

plot   the events that happen in the story

point of view   the perspective from which a story is presented to a reader

protagonist   the main character, usually the hero

rhythm   the beat or meter of a poem

satire   the ridicule of a subject

simile   a comparison of two things using the words "like" or "as"

soliloquy   a speech addressed to the audience where one character expounds upon his predicament

stage directions   authorial instructions inserted in parentheses to tell the actor or director how to act, move, or speak

stanza   a section of lines in a poem

style   the author's unique manner of expression; the author's voice

surrealism/theater of the absurd a style of play that doesn't have a logical progression of narrative or a clear sequence of events or theme

tense time perspective from which a piece is written (past, present, or future)

theme the main idea of a piece of literature

tone the style or manner of expression

tragedy a play that is sad or addresses sorrowful or difficult themes

voice the perspective from which a piece is written, most often first-person or third-person

Chapter 11
Answers and
Explanations to Drills

CHAPTER 5

Drill #1

Page 29

Question	Explanation
Answers will vary, but here are some possibilities.	
24	What happens when the birds see the hunter?
49	What's the "grand caper"?
30	What does "favored" mean in this context?

Drill #2

Page 34

Question	Explanation
What are the eight steps for tackling questions?	
1	Look at the date.
2	Read the passage.
3	Decide which question to do first.
4	Cover the answers.
5	Translate the question.
6	Go back to the passage.
7	Find the answer, and translate it into your own words.
8	POE.
What are the three kinds of questions on the SAT Literature Subject Test?	
1	specific
2	general
2	weird
What are the two kinds of weird questions on the SAT Literature Subject Test?	
1	NOT/LEAST/EXCEPT
2	Roman numeral

CHAPTER 6

Drill #1

Page 43

Metaphor	Simile	Personification/Anthropomorphism
4	1	2
7	3	5
9	8	6
		10

Drill #2

Page 44

Onomatopoeia	Alliteration	Oxymoron	Pathos
2	4	3	1
7	8	5	6
10		9	

Drill #4

Pages 46–47

Question	Answer	Explanation
1	D	The sentence, when pared down, is "None of these things shall content my musing mind," so the correct answer is (D). None of the other answer choices contain the main verb.
2	C	The voice is not compared to a woodcock, but rather the "calling" of a woodcock (line 15) (C). The voice is compared to the stream (lines 11–12) (A). The voice is compared to the wind (line 14) (B) and woodcock music (line 16) (D). The voice is compared to children's feet in line 18 (E).
3	C	The author is calling the sun "faithful"—a human characteristic, so this is an example of personification (C). It is not ironic or paradoxical (A), (B). There is no contradiction, so it is not an oxymoron (D). Poetic license is when a writer ignores conventional form or fact to achieve a desired effect. This is not the case here (E).

Question	Answer	Explanation
4	B	The title of the poem is "Elegy," so we can assume it's written as an elegy (B). The meter is not regular throughout the poem (A), and the rhyme scheme varies (C). There is no extended allegory (D), and the author is not asking for empathy (E).

CHAPTER 7

Drill #1

Pages 55–56

Question		Explanation
What is the effect of the use of the first person?		First-person narrative makes the story more personal but gives you just one perspective.
Where is the metaphor? What is the effect of using a metaphor?		Metaphor: "November in my soul." Effect: bringing to life a vivid image.
What is your impression of the narrator?		Insightful and interesting, but a rather unhappy character.
1	B	The author is introducing the character here, and the informal voice as well as the actions are humorous (B). There is no complete background (for example, we don't know where the narrator was born) (A). The setting is not a major part of the passage (C). There is nothing foreshadowed (D), and the main purpose of the passage is not to state the character's profession (that takes only one word, not a whole paragraph) (E).
2	C	For the narrator, sailing is the way he gets rid of his melancholy ("growing grim about the mouth . . . a damp, drizzly November in my soul") (C). An old-fashioned meaning of spleen is "melancholy." Spleen does not mean "path" (A), nor does it refer to the circulation of blood (B). Although a spleen is an organ, the word does not refer to a body part in this context, and it's not a kidney (D). There is no evidence that the narrator needs to drive off excess energy (E).

Drill #2

Pages 57–58

Question	Answer	Explanation
What is the effect of the third-person voice in the description?		The third person has the effect of making it a more objective description. This third person, you may notice, is simply describing the action that takes place, not really getting into the minds of the characters.
Is the description emotional or objective?		The description is very objective.
Where is the metaphor, and what is the purpose of it?		Metaphor: "the way a bear drags his paws." Effect: providing an image of the character.
1	A	The characters' similarities are described, followed by their differences (A). The characters are not introduced separately (B). Only the second character is compared to an animal (C). The faces are not described until after their clothes are (D). There are no inner thoughts (E).
2	B	The tone is one of neutrality—an unbiased narrator describing the action (B). There is no contempt (A). Although they are described, "scrutiny" is too strong a word (C). There is nothing supernatural about the passage (D). There is no inquiry (E).

Drill #3

Page 59

Question	Answer	Explanation
1	A	The narrator is making fun of the notion that everyone is equal (A). He is not harsh (B), nor is the narrative dark (C). There is no emotion in the narration (D), and the narration is not too casual (E).
2	B	The author uses repetition to underscore his point that everyone is equal (B). The repetition does not introduce a theme (A). The repetition is not intended to make the reader lonely (C). There is no commonly held assumption that is refuted (D). The three elements introduced are not contradictory (E)
3	D	The repetition of the subject "nobody" is an example of parallelism (D). There is no internal rhyme (A), and he does not mimic lower-class speech (B). The comparison is not general (C). The protagonist is not mentioned in the first passage (E).

Drill #4

Page 61

Question	Answer	Explanation
1	C	Marguerite's name doesn't sound familiar; that is stage fright (C). There is nothing to tell us if she had graduated before (A). She had made "preparations," so she is not surprised (B). She did get her diploma and sat down (D). There is no evidence that she is a painter (E).
2	E	The sentence refers to an Amazon, so it is an allusion (E). The author is not intruding here (A). There is no anachronism (B). The syntax is different, yes, but not complicated (C). There is no evidence of anthropomorphism here (D).

Drill #5

Pages 62–64

Question	Answer	Explanation
1	C	Lin is thumbing through a book while everyone else is working, so the contrast is between intellect and physicality (C). There is nothing exactly central or peripheral (A). There is no mention of anyone corrupt or honest (B). There is no mention of heaven (D), so secular and divine are not mentioned either (E).
2	D	Lin keeps looking around; he cannot concentrate on his book, and his mind wanders, so (D) is the best answer. He is not "haughty" (A), nor is he indifferent to his surroundings (B). He does not ask any questions (C). "Enthralled" is too strong a word for the curiosity he feels (E).
3	B	The fact that the house is the same as it was twenty years ago and the books are mildewed suggests that Lin has been away a long time (B). We do not know his profession (A) or the purpose for his visit (C). He is comfortable, so he is used to the country (D), and it is not clear that the landscape is beautiful (E).
4	D	Bellows do not cough, so this is an example of personification (D). Cucumbers can hang (A), chickens strut, and geese waddle (B). Air can reek (C), and sows can oink (E).

5	A	The character is speaking to himself without quotes, so Statement I is true. The narrator continues speaking about the books, so there is no shift, so II is false. We do not know if Lin is relinquishing his pastoral life, so Statement III is not true.
6	C	The "distillers' grains mixed in the pig feed" cause the sour smell (C), not the cooking (A), nor the manure (B). The mildewed books do not smell (D), nor does the field (E).
7	C	The passage describes Lin's home in detail (C). It is not a paean (hymn of praise) (A) or an elegy for a previous time (B). The character does not experience an epiphany (D). There is no evident allegory (E).

Drill #6

Pages 65–66

Question	Answer	Explanation
1	C	Mrs. Penniman is in charge of Catherine's lessons, so "supervising" is a good synonym (C). She does not ignore her talent (A), nor does she teach Catherine herself (B). She encourages Catherine (D). We don't know who hires Catherine's tutors (E).
2	B	"It is I who supply the butter," says Mrs. Penniman (B). Secrets are compared to addled eggs (A). "Bread" is compared to goodness, not Mrs. Penniman's influence (C). "The salt of malice" is a phrase and is not being used as a symbol (D). Mrs. Penniman's influence is not compared to a fool (E).
3	E	In contrast to her piano talent, Catherine was just fair as a dancer (E). There is no mention of Catherine's appearance (A). We don't know if she is aware of her talent (B) or if it is in her character to brag (C). She was not a talented dancer (D).
4	E	The narration is observant of Catherine's qualities and Mrs. Penniman's thoughts (E). It is not melodramatic (A), nor is there any evidence of irony (B). It is not sardonic (meanly satiric) (C), nor is it particularly didactic (designed to instruct) (D).
5	A	The point of view is of an omniscient narrator (A). We don't know who the protagonist is (B). There is no use of the second-person "you" (C) or of first-person "I" (D) and (E).
6	E	In this passage secrets are compared to "addled eggs." Secrets are impractical—rotten is the best answer because none of the other words has a negative connotation (E). They are not "confused" (A); this is the first definition for "addled," not the meaning in this passage. Rotten eggs may be useless, but that is not the meaning of addled (B). There is nothing to suggest that scrambled eggs are impractical (C). Don't confuse "addled" with "saddled" (D).

CHAPTER 8

Drill #1

Page 72

Question	Answer	Explanation
What is the poem about?		A guy who doesn't want his beloved to leave in the morning.
Who is the narrator of this poem?		The narrator is someone who is in love.
What do we know about the narrator?		The narrator is a pilgrim who has to be parted from his lover.
What do we know about the beloved in this poem?		Not a whole heck of a lot. She has bright eyes.
Is there a pattern of rhyme and meter?		Yes, the poem has regular meter and an obvious rhyme scheme: AA, BB, CC.
1	B	There is an obvious rhyme scheme: AA, BB, CC, so (B) is the correct answer. There is no onomatopoeia (A) nor oxymoron (C). The perspective does not change (D), and there is no paradox that remains unsolved (E).
2	E	He says her eyes give off light, and she gives him joy (E). He's happy (E). We don't know that it's not really morning (A). We don't know about the consequences of being discovered (B). We don't know what the woman will do (C). We don't know where the speaker of the poem is (D).

Drill #2

Pages 75–78

Question	Answer	Explanation
What are some examples of alliteration?		"dimes" and "dollars," "buys shoes for the baby," "bright bowl of brass is beautiful"
Which words are repeated? Why do you think the author does this?		The money denominations are repeated, as is the word "boy!" and the word "spittoon." The author probably does this to emphasize the words and impart the themes of the poem: The man is concerned with earning enough money to provide for his family. The appellation of "boy" grates on him, and his job polishing spittoons all day is monotonous.
Where does the author use allusion?		Kings David and Solomon (lines 33–34)
1	C	Alliteration is definitely used, so (C) is the answer. There is no analogy (A). He is not describing a scene in church (B). The brass is compared to symbols; the bowls are not (D). The poem never talks about poetry (E).
2	C	The author lists the cities to imply that the narrator could be any man in any city (C). There is no evidence that the narrator is educated in geography (A). There is no evidence of a newspaper in the poem (B). There is no extended analogy (D). The cities do not function as symbols (E).
3	A	There is personification and alliteration in this line, but it is obviously intentional and not haphazard, so the answer is (A), not (B). Nothing is repeated (C). Although two dollars does involve economics, this is not the purpose of the phrase (D). There is no allusion (E).
4	C	The narrator is a man who cleans spittoons in hotels for a living. He dedicates his work to God, so he is proud. He is not in charge (A). He is not the one tipping (B). He is not outspoken as a critic (D). There is no evidence he is stingy, just poor (E).
5	D	The narrator works hard to polish the spittoons to provide for his family (D). He may be reverent, but we have no examples of his honesty (A). He is not selfish (B). We don't know if he is ignorant (C). The narrator has a family, so he is not childlike. Being called "boy" is an insult (E).
6	E	At the end of the poem we know a lot about this narrator and what motivates him, so (E) is the best answer. There is no nature in the poem (A). Places are not described (B). The poem is not an allegory (C). The poem is not trying to teach something (D).
7	E	The rhythm at the beginning mimics the polishing motion of the narrator as he cleans spittoons, so Statement I is true. The secular (cleaning) is short and staccato, while the divine (the religious imagery) is characterized by longer, more flowing sentences, so Statement II is true. And the rhythm makes the poem melodious, so Statement III is true.

Question	Answer	Explanation
8	E	The poem ends with the speaker finding meaning in his job because he does it for God (E). The poem does not say the situation is hopeless (A). The man finds meaning, so the job is not empty (B). The narrator's faith does not waiver (C). There is nothing that says he will persevere (D).
9	B	The lines are spoken by the boss. They are a command for the narrator's attention and are derogatory because they call him "boy" and don't address him by name (B). The speaker does not talk to his son (A). The boss is calling the narrator, not greeting him (C). It is not urban slang (D). The speaker's conscience is not in the poem (E).
10	A	The cities mentioned and the difficult situation of the narrator mean that poverty is tough (A). It does not mention thriftiness (B); rather, it talks about poverty. We don't know when brass was discovered (C). Imagination is not talked about as a means of escape (D). We don't know that good things will come to the narrator (E).

Drill #3

Pages 79–81

Question	Answer	Explanation
What are the examples of similes?		"frigate like a book," "coursers like a page"
What are the examples of metaphors?		"books as chariots," "reading as a traverse"
What is an example of personification?		"prancing poetry"
Is there rhythm and meter? Describe.		There is a regular meter and a rhyme scheme. We can guess that it is a traditional form. It's a little sing-songy, so it is probably not a poem about death.
What do you think is the main idea of the poem?		No journey is as cool or as inexpensive as reading a book.
1	D	Books are great for learning about other cultures—better than boats and horses, according to the author (D). The author is comparing boats to books, so (A) is not correct. The author prefers books for the mind rather than boats or horses for the body (B). There is no mention of the number of books or boats (C). There is no evidence that the author values the practical or doesn't value the frivolous (E).
2	A	We know from the fact that they are "prancing" that coursers are probably horses (A). "Skiffs" don't prance (B). "Textbooks" are not mentioned in the poem (C). "Ancient chariots" cannot prance (D). The coursers are things that carry people, so they can't be "poetic devices" (E).

Question	Answer	Explanation
3	B	The words in the poem are pretty high falutin': "coursers," "frigates" (B). There are not a lot of description words (A) or forceful actions (C). There is no humorous word play (D). The contrasts are not awkward (E).
4	C	Even the poorest can take a journey into a book without having to pay for it (C). There is no mention of which economic group travels more (A). There is no suggestion to how to spend money (B). There is no discussion of how much books should cost (D). The author doesn't go so far as to talk about readers' souls (E).
5	B	The speaker thinks reading is better than traveling, so the written word must have great power (B). There is no discussion of action versus passivity (A). We don't know what kinds of books the speaker likes to read (C). We don't know for sure that the speaker likes to fantasize (D). There is no mention of virtue (E).
6	C	The poem is about how nothing is quite like the adventure of reading (C). The poem is not about the journey of life (A), nor is it about wisdom (B). There is nothing in the poem about education (D) or about the aging process (E).
7	D	The speaker is trying to gently convince us about how great it is to read (D). There is not a lecture (A), nor is the speaker forceful (B). The speaker is not proactive (C), nor is she selfish (E).

Drill #4

Pages 82–84

Question	Answer	Explanation
1	E	The author employs all of these techniques, but nowhere makes reference to the Bible (E). There is expressive use of punctuation marks, especially exclamation points, throughout (A). The rhyme scheme is regular: AA, BB, CC, DD, EE, FF, etc. (B), and each of the lines has the same number of syllables (7), making the meter regular (C). There are many adjectives: "fond," "seraphic," etc. (D).
2	C	The narrator is mocking death by saying that he's heard so much about its sting and questioning where it is (C). The question is not harsh (A). The question is not curious or doubtful (B). The question is not earnest—the narrator is not really looking for death's sting (D). There is no paradox in the question (E).
3	D	"Sounds," in this case, is a noun, not a verb (D). All of the other answers are active verbs (A), (B), (C), and (E).

Question	Answer	Explanation
4	A	In the first stanza the narrator talks to nature; in the second, he talks to his soul, and in the third, he asks the angels to lend him their wings (A). He does not talk about life after death (although he can see heaven, he does not talk about what life will be like there) (B). The first stanza says that death is blissful as well as painful (C). The speaker is the same throughout the poem (D). The second stanza does not taunt death, and the third stanza is not reluctant (E).
5	E	The speaker is asking death to take him from his body (E). "Frame" is not a picture of the world (A) or any previously held image (B). (C) is a too-literal interpretation of the word. The speaker does not talk about the frame as metaphor, but rather the literal frame of the body (D).
6	A	Death may be painful (loss of sense, etc.) but it is blissful, too (A). Death has no victory ("where is thy victory?") (B). He does not talk of resisting death (C). There is no notion that the next life will be better (D). There is no talk of the eternity of death (E).
7	D	The descriptions of death's symptoms and how death affects his body are elaborate (D). Romance is not a theme in the poem (A). The poem is not playful (B), nor is it harshly critical (C). The poem is emotionally expressive, not cryptic (hard to understand) (E).
8	B	The last lines underscore that death is less about physical pain and more about mental bliss (B). Death does hurt (A). There is no battle being fought (C). The speaker does not have an antagonistic relationship with death (D). Death is not transient (E).

Drill #5

Pages 85–86

Question	Answer	Explanation
1	C	"Silver" and "sound" are alliterative (C). There is no comparison between silver and gold (A). "Silver" does not foreshadow the hunt (B). Silver is not necessarily bright (D). The horn is not about wealth, nor are we told it's beautiful (E).
2	D	Like the hounds howling at the moon, the sounds are onomatopoetic (D). No one is greeting anyone in the poem (A). There is no suggestion that the author means to use the word "hollow" (B). There is no evidence that there is a physical spot to echo back (no cave or canyon) (C). The word "halo" does not make sense in this context (E).
3	B	The author is persuading the reader gently but firmly (B). The author is not "hostile" (A). The author is not trying to teach a lesson (C). The author has written three stanzas; clearly she is not ambivalent (D). There is no evidence of disgust in the poem (E).

Question	Answer	Explanation
4	A	The poem is about someone who has gotten so caught up in his or her empty life that he or she has forgotten what is really important (A). There is no evidence of shame in the poem (B). The wealth is simply a metaphor. Plus, we don't know if perhaps the person was wealthy all of his or her life (C). There is no suggestion in the poem that the addressee is about to die (D). Vanity is not mentioned in the poem (E).
5	B	In the poem, the speaker addresses someone who has lost touch with what is important in life, so Statement II is true. The madman's song does not mean that he or she was committed to an asylum, so Statement I is not true. The person to whom the poem is addressed is someone who has lost passion, not someone who is filled with it, so Statement III is not true.
6	B	The repetition in the poem is of the passionate actions—following, hallo-ing, etc.—so it mimics the poem's theme of finding passion. It does not necessarily help the rhyme scheme (A). The reader is not punished (C). There is no anger in the poem (D). The person addressed is not lazy, but rather passionless (E).

CHAPTER 9

Drill #1

Pages 92–93

Question	Answer	Explanation
1	C	Mrs. Pearce never is contrasted with the king (C). Eliza was a flower girl—Higgins is hoping to make her into a lady in a florist's shop (A). If she's good, she goes to the palace; if she's bad, she goes to jail in the Tower of London (B). Again, good = proper bedroom. Bad = kitchen (D). Goodness is contrasted with naughtiness (E).
2	E	Higgins considers Eliza as someone he can just boss around because she's stupid (E). He does not necessarily think she is willful, and he knows she's not a child (A). She is not a servant because she won't have to do chores (B). He looks down on her; we know she is not a potential wife because of the risks and rewards Higgins lays out for her. Plus, matrimony is never mentioned (C). If it were futile, he would not embark on the project (D).
3	E	According to Higgins, she will work in a florist's shop as a lady, so she will have to work (E). Ladies "speak beautifully" (A) and are like "a lady in a florist's shop" (B). She will ride in taxis (private transportation), not buses or trolleys (public) (C). Ladies are "beautifully dressed" (D).

Question	Answer	Explanation
4	B	Eliza can utter only unintelligible sounds, while Higgins speechifies (B). The amount of dialogue does not prove that they are not equal (A). The amount of dialogue does not show the extent of Higgins's prejudice (C), nor does it show his opinion of Eliza's abilities (D). It also does not show Eliza's inability to follow Higgins's instructions (E).
5	A	Higgins oversimplifies the matter and talks to Eliza as though she were a child (A). He is not trying to teach her something with the speech (B), (C), nor does the speech really explain anything (D). His words are not persuasive (E).
6	B	Eliza is described as "overwhelmed." There is no mention of her insecurity (A). Although she may feel confused, it is not supported in the passage (C). There is no mention of her feeling ineffectual (D) or insignificant (E).

Drill #2

Pages 94–97

Question	Answer	Explanation
1	D	Coyle is bringing up bills from various merchants who are going to take action against Sir Edward because he hasn't paid them, so a judge's decision and a court order are the best paraphrase (D). No one is being branded a criminal (A). The actions are real, not just moral (B). There is no suggestion of a partnership (C). There is no reference to a search of the property (E).
2	A	Coyle manages Sir Edward's accounts as his "agent" or money manager (A). He is not a lawyer (B). Although Coyle is employed by Sir Edward, he is not a servant (C). Sir Edward's father was a benefactor for Coyle's father, but the current generation does not have this arrangement (D). Coyle and Sir Edward are not related, although Coyle wants to marry Sir Edward's daughter (E).
3	A	Coyle's father lent Sir Edward's father money and took a property as an assurance that he would pay Coyle's father back, which never happened. In this situation, the property is collateral (A). "Agreement" does not describe the role of the property (B), nor does assurance have the precise meaning (C). Security does not mean "welfare" (D), nor is the property a prize (E).
4	C	Sir Edward calls the debts "extortion," which means he thinks they are unfair (C). "Infernal" is merely an insult, not a comment on the fairness of the bills (A). "Confound" is an expletive like "darn" (B). "Impudence" describes Coyle's attitude, not the situation (D). "Unencumbered" in this context means "available to mortgage," which does not fit the situation (E).

Question	Answer	Explanation
5	B	Coyle offers to keep "the Ravensdale estate in the family" if Sir Edward will give Coyle his daughter (B). Coyle does not offer to pay off the creditors—his offer extends only to Ravensdale (A). Coyle wants to marry Sir Edward's daughter, not the residents (C). Coyle does not want to marry Sir Edward's daughter to prevent her financial ruin (D). There is no love affair between Coyle and Sir Edward's daughter ("Florence detests him") (E).
6	D	Sir Edward appears to argue with himself, here, voicing both sides of the argument to accept or deny Coyle's offer. The lines are not quite a monologue, nor do they express doubt (A). Just because the character is talking to himself does not mean he's going mad (B). The character is not addressing the audience (C). The lines do not explain a plot point; they merely follow Sir Edward's reasoning.

Part III
The Princeton Review Practice SAT Literature Subject Tests

Chapter 12
How to Take the Practice
SAT Literature Subject Tests

TAKING THE PRACTICE TESTS

Try to re-create test conditions as closely as possible. This means no water breaks, no IM breaks, and no yelling-at-your-little-brother breaks. Sit down in a place where you won't be interrupted and get a reliable watch or clock to measure one hour. Cross off answers as you eliminate them, and practice bubbling your answers on the sheet provided after each test. If you do this, you'll get a good idea of how the test works and what you need to improve upon.

As you take the test, mark questions that you guessed on with a "G." This will help you gauge how well you're guessing.

After Each Practice Test, Ask Yourself . . .

Did You Run Out of Time?

If you ran out of time and didn't get to a few easy questions at the end of the test, you're not discriminating enough when it comes to skipping questions. Don't linger in any one place too long—one question is never worth five minutes of your time.

> 60 minutes for 61–63 questions = < 1 minute per question

Skip Around
Don't forget to skip around. Do the easy questions first; then go back to the hard ones.

Did You Get a Lot of "Easy" Questions Wrong?

Sometimes, when you look back and review, you can't believe you got such an easy question wrong. Slow down. Did you read the question correctly the first time around? Did you pick the right answer but circle an incorrect choice? Rushing is the major cause of avoidable errors.

Whoa, Nelly!
Don't rush. This only results in careless errors.

Did You Mismark Answers on Your Answer Sheet?

It's pretty easy to mismark answers when you're skipping around (as you should be). Don't forget to pick a bubbling method (discussed in Chapter 2) and stick with it. It is really a huge bummer if you get the answers right but don't get credit because you filled in the wrong bubble.

Assessing Your Performance

Don't just sit back and drink a glass of lemonade after you complete your practice test. Study your results so you can improve your score. Fill in the lines below. It'll help . . . really.

1. How many easy questions did you get wrong? (Easy questions are the ones you can't believe you got wrong.)

   _____

2. Why did you get these wrong? (Maybe you didn't read the question closely enough, didn't read the right place in the passage, or misread the answer choices.)

   _____

   _____

3. How many hard questions did you get wrong? (Hard questions are the ones you really have to study to understand why the right answer is right.)

   _____

4. How many questions did you guess on?

   _____

5. How many of those did you get right?

   _____

   Wrong?

   _____

6. If you got the guessed answers wrong, did you narrow down the answer choices to two or three (or even four)?

   _____

   Was the right answer among those?

   _____

   If so, guessing was the right move. How can you improve your guessing?

   _____

7. Did you feel more comfortable with the poetry or the prose?

   _____

8. What parts of the book should you go over again before you take the next practice test or the real SAT Literature Subject Test?

   _____

Chapter 13
Practice Test 1

PRACTICE SAT LITERATURE
SUBJECT TEST 1

TEST 1

Your responses to the SAT Literature Subject Test questions should be filled in on Test 1 of your answer sheet.

LITERATURE TEST 1

Directions: This test consists of selections from literary works and questions on their content, form, and style. After reading each passage or poem, choose the best answer to each question and fill in the corresponding oval on the answer sheet.

Note: Pay particular attention to questions that contain the words NOT, LEAST, or EXCEPT.

Questions 1-9. Read the following passage carefully before you choose your answers.

Maman-Nainaine said that when the figs were ripe Babette might go to visit her cousins down on the Bayou-Lafourche where the sugar cane grows. Not that the ripening of figs had the least thing to
5   do with it, but that is the way Maman-Nainaine was.

It seemed to Babette a very long time to wait; for the leaves upon the trees were tender yet, and the figs were like little hard green marbles.
10   But warm rains came along and plenty of strong sunshine, and though Maman-Nainaine was as patient as the statue of la Madone, and Babette as restless as a hummingbird, the first thing they both knew it was hot summertime. Every day
15   Babette danced out to where the fig-trees were in a long line against the fence. She walked slowly beneath them, carefully peering between the gnarled, spreading branches. But each time she came disconsolate away again. What she saw there
20   finally was something that made her sing and dance the whole long day.

When Maman-Nainaine sat down in her stately way to breakfast the following morning, her muslin cap standing like an aureole about her
25   white, placid face, Babette approached. She bore a dainty porcelain platter, which she set down before her godmother. It contained a dozen purple figs, fringed around with their rich green leaves.

"Ah," said Maman-Nainaine arching her
30   eyebrows, "how early the figs have ripened this year!"

"Oh," said Babette. "I think they have ripened very late."

"Babette," continued Maman-Nainaine, as she
35   peeled the very plumpest figs with her pointed silver fruit-knife, "you will carry my love to them all down on Bayou-Lafourche. And tell your Tante Frosine I shall look for her at Toussaint—when the chrysanthemums are in bloom."

(1893)

1. In the passage, the ripening figs are symbolic of

    (A) the fruits of labor
    (B) the maturation of Babette
    (C) the difficulty of life
    (D) the enigma of nature
    (E) the battle between Maman-Nainaine and Babette

2. The phrase "but that is the way Maman-Nainaine was" suggests which of the following about Maman-Nainaine?

    (A) She was not aware of the seriousness of the situation.
    (B) She was an overly strict woman.
    (C) Her actions had their own logic.
    (D) She doled out punishment for no reason.
    (E) Figs were her favorite fruit.

3. What is the effect of the disagreement (lines 1-6)?

    (A) It illustrates Maman-Nainaine's bad judgment.
    (B) It serves to illustrate the patience of Maman-Nainaine and the impatience of Babette.
    (C) It demonstrates a passage of time.
    (D) It makes Babette appear spoiled and insolent.
    (E) It shows how argumentative Babette can be.

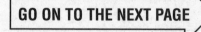
GO ON TO THE NEXT PAGE

4. In the passage, Maman-Nainaine's attitude toward Babette can best be characterized as

   (A) contemptuous
   (B) flippant
   (C) reluctantly accepting
   (D) joyously optimistic
   (E) wisely patient

5. All of the following pairs of words illustrate the difference between Maman-Nainaine and Babette EXCEPT

   (A) "patient" (line 12) and "restless" (line 13)
   (B) "early" (line 30) and "late" (line 33)
   (C) "purple" (line 27) and "green" (line 28)
   (D) "danced" (line 15) and "sat" (line 22)
   (E) "ripe" (line 2) and "bloom" (line 39)

6. Which is the effect of the last sentence of the passage?

   (A) It shows that Maman-Nainaine is clearly illogical.
   (B) It serves as ironic counterpoint to the rest of the story.
   (C) It advances the symbolism introduced with the ripened figs.
   (D) It introduces a literary allusion.
   (E) It advances the story beyond its scope.

7. Maman-Nainaine's peeling of "the very plumpest figs" (line 35) illustrates that Maman-Nainaine

   (A) is testing their ripeness
   (B) prefers to cook her own food
   (C) is superstitious
   (D) is a refined woman
   (E) enjoys making fun of Babette

8. The word "though" (line 11) implies which of the following in the context of the sentence?

   (A) The two women were in disagreement.
   (B) Patience is a virtue when waiting for something.
   (C) Figs were not really important.
   (D) Their patience and impatience had no effect on nature.
   (E) Maman-Nainaine's patience was annoying to Babette.

9. The narrative point of view of the passage as a whole is that of

   (A) a disapproving observer
   (B) a first-person impartial observer
   (C) the protagonist
   (D) an unreliable narrator
   (E) a third-person objective observer

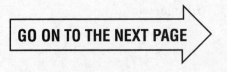

GO ON TO THE NEXT PAGE

Questions 10-18. Read the following poem carefully before you choose your answers.

"On His Deceased Wife"

Methought I saw my late espoused Saint
   Brought to me like Alcestis from the grave,
   Whom Jove's great son to her glad husband gave,
   Rescu'd from death by force though pale and faint.
5 Mine as whom wash't from spot of childbed taint,
   Purification in the old law did save,
   And such, as yet once more I trust to have
   Full sight of her in Heaven without restraint,
Came vested all in white, pure as her mind:
10 Her face was vail'd, yet to my fancied sight,
   Love, sweetness, goodness, in her person shin'd
So clear, as in no face with more delight.
   But O, as to embrace me she inclined
   I wak'd, she fled, and day brought back my night.

(1658)

10. "Whom Jove's's great son" (line 3) acts as which of the following?

   (A) a play on words
   (B) a contradiction
   (C) hyperbole
   (D) mythological allusion
   (E) allegory

11. Line 4 refers to which of the following?

   I. "my late espoused Saint" (line 1)
   II. "Alcestis" (line 2)
   III. "her glad husband" (line 3)

   (A) I only
   (B) II only
   (C) I and II only
   (D) I and III only
   (E) II and III only

12. In context, the word "save" (line 6) means which of the following?

   (A) preserve
   (B) keep in health
   (C) deliver from sin and punishment
   (D) rescue from harm
   (E) maintain

13. The purpose of the last line is to suggest

   (A) a contrast between dreaming and waking states
   (B) the poet's depression
   (C) an allusion to the sonnet form
   (D) a parallel to the opening quatrain
   (E) that the writer is optimistic about the future

14. In context, "my fancied sight" (line 10) suggests that the author is

   (A) imbuing his deceased wife with qualities she did not have
   (B) unable to separate reality from dreams
   (C) capriciously conjuring up his wife's image
   (D) dreaming
   (E) suffering from delusions

GO ON TO THE NEXT PAGE

15. The author's attitude toward his wife can best be described as

(A) inconsolable
(B) reverential
(C) hopeful
(D) incongruous
(E) obsequious

16. The poem is primarily concerned with

(A) the mourning process
(B) the struggle against dying
(C) the injustice of death
(D) the nature of immortality
(E) a belief in heaven

17. What is the effect of using the word "glad" (line 3) instead of "happy" or "joyous"?

(A) It suggests that the husband is overwhelmed.
(B) It links to "great" and "gave" by alliteration.
(C) It stresses that the husband is a particular person.
(D) It distinguishes between "Jove's great son" and the husband.
(E) It alludes to "I" in line 1.

18. Which of the following are terms of opposition in the poem?

(A) "embrace" and "inclined" (line 13)
(B) "day" and "night" (line 14)
(C) "Full sight" and "without restraint" (line 8)
(D) "wash't" (line 5) and "Purification" (line 6)
(E) "sight" (line 10) and "shin'd" (line 11)

Questions 19-27. Read the following passage carefully before you choose your answers.

Keenly alive to this prejudice of hers, Mr. Keeble stopped after making his announcement, and had to rattle the keys in his pocket in order to acquire the necessary courage to continue.
5 He was not looking at his wife, but knew just how forbidding her expression must be. This task of his was no easy, congenial task for a pleasant summer morning.

"She says in her letter," proceeded
10 Mr. Keeble, his eyes on the carpet and his cheeks a deeper pink, "that young Jackson has got the chance of buying a big farm . . . in Lincolnshire, I think she said . . . if he can raise three thousand pounds."
15 He paused, and stole a glance at his wife. It was as he had feared. She had congealed. Like some spell, the name had apparently turned her to marble. It was like the Pygmalion and Galatea business working the wrong way round.
20 She was presumably breathing, but there was no sign of it.

"So I was just thinking," said Mr. Keeble, producing another *obbligato* on the keys, "it just crossed my mind . . . it isn't as if the thing
25 were speculation . . . the place is apparently coining money . . . present owner only selling because he wants to go abroad . . . it occurred to me . . . and they would pay good interest on the loan . . ."
30 "What loan?" enquired the statue icily, coming to life.

(1924)

19. Which of the following is the intended effect of the pauses in Mr. Keeble's conversation?

(A) It demonstrates that he is a feeble man.
(B) It makes his speech disjointed.
(C) It shows his hesitancy in approaching his wife.
(D) It slows the rhythm of the conversation.
(E) It elucidates his main point.

20. Which of the following expresses a mythological allusion made in the passage?

(A) "interest on the loan" (lines 28-29)
(B) "no sign of it" (lines 20-21)
(C) "turned her to marble" (lines 17-18)
(D) "in Lincolnshire" (lines 12-13)
(E) "the Pygmalion and Galatea business" (lines 18-19)

21. All of the following represent metaphors or similes used by the authors EXCEPT

(A) "She had congealed" (line 16)
(B) "enquired the statue icily" (line 30)
(C) "coming to life" (line 31)
(D) "presumably breathing" (line 20)
(E) "Like some spell" (lines 16-17)

22. The phrase "the place is apparently coining money" (lines 25-26) is meant to imply

(A) the farm is presently engaged in illegal activities
(B) the farm is profitable
(C) the investment is unnecessary
(D) the farm serves as a bank for the local people
(E) Lincolnshire is a profitable place to live

23. Which of the following expresses Mr. Keeble's wife's feeling toward the loan?

(A) amused detachment
(B) utter disgust
(C) preformed opposition
(D) blatant apathy
(E) neutrality

GO ON TO THE NEXT PAGE

24. All of the following are physical manifestations of Mr. Keeble's anticipation of his wife's response EXCEPT

    (A) "Keenly alive" (line 1)
    (B) "had to rattle the keys" (line 3)
    (C) "was not looking at his wife" (line 5)
    (D) "his eyes on the carpet" (line 10)
    (E) "producing another *obbligato*" (line 23)

25. The phrase "in Lincolnshire, I think she said" (lines 12-13) implies that which of the following is true of Keeble?

    (A) Keeble is unaware of the location of the farm.
    (B) Keeble thinks the location is unimportant.
    (C) Keeble's memory is failing.
    (D) Keeble is attempting to appear casual.
    (E) Keeble wants to conceal the location from his wife.

26. Keeble's relationship with his wife is such that

       I. he needs her approval
      II. he is disgusted by her
     III. he is intimidated by her

    (A) II only
    (B) III only
    (C) I and III only
    (D) II and III only
    (E) I, II, and III

27. The last line implies which of the following?

    (A) Mr. Keeble's wife is not interested in lending him money.
    (B) Mr. Keeble's wife is interested in the proposition.
    (C) Mr. Keeble has succeeded in his mission.
    (D) Mr. Keeble's wife is keeping an open mind about the loan.
    (E) Mr. Keeble's wife wants to hear more about the loan.

GO ON TO THE NEXT PAGE

Questions 28-37. Read the following passage carefully before you choose your answers.

[*A street in London*]

Enter LORD MAYOR *(Sir Roger Otley) and* EARL OF LINCOLN

LINC: My Lord Mayor, you have sundry times
　　　Feasted myself, and many courtiers more;
　　　Seldom or never can we be so kind
　　　To make requital of your courtesy.
5　　But, leaving this, I hear my cousin Lacy
　　　Is much affected to your daughter Rose.

L. MAYOR: True, my good Lord, and she loves him so well
　　　That I mislike her boldness in the chase.

10　LINC: Why, my Lord Mayor, think you it then a shame
　　　To join a Lacy with an Otley's name?

L. MAYOR: Too mean is my poor girl for his high birth;
　　　Poor citizens must not with courtiers wed,
15　　Who will in silks and gay apparel spend
　　　More in one year than I am worth by far;
　　　Therefore your honour need not doubt my girl.

LINC: Take heed, my Lord, advise you what you do;
　　　A verier unthrift lives not in the world
20　　Than is my cousin; for I'll tell you what,
　　　'Tis now almost a year since he requested
　　　To travel countries for experience;
　　　I furnish'd him with coin, bills of exchange,
　　　Letters of credit, men to wait on him,
25　　Solicited my friends in Italy
　　　Well to respect him; but to see the end:
　　　Scant had he journey'd through half Germany,
　　　But all his coin was spent, his men cast off,
　　　His bills embezzl'd, and my jolly coz,
30　　Asham'd to show his bankrupt presence here,
　　　Became a shoemaker in Wittenberg.
　　　A goodly science for a gentleman
　　　Of such descent! Now judge the rest by this:
　　　Suppose your daughter have a thousand pound,
35　　He did consume me more in one half-year;
　　　And make him heir to all the wealth you have,
　　　One twelvemonth's rioting will waste it all.
　　　Then seek, my Lord, some honest citizen
　　　To wed your daughter to.

40　L. MAYOR: I thank your lordship.
　　　(*Aside.*) Well, fox, I understand your subtlety.—
　　　As for your nephew, let your lordship's eye
　　　But watch his actions, and you need not fear,
　　　For I have sent my daughter far enough.
45　　And yet your cousin Rowland might do well
　　　Now he hath learn'd an occupation;
　　　(*Aside.*) And yet I scorn to call him son-in-law.

LINC: Ay, but I have a better trade for him;
　　　I thank His Grace he hath appointed him
50　　Chief colonel of all those companies
　　　Muster'd in London and the shires about
　　　To serve His Highness in those wars of France.
　　　See where he comes.

(1599)

28. The word "sundry" (line 1) most nearly means

(A) groceries
(B) numerous
(C) provisions
(D) infrequent
(E) few

29. The main effect of the Earl of Lincoln's first four lines is to

(A) return Lord Mayor's generosity
(B) acknowledge his indebtedness to Lord Mayor
(C) emphasize the differences between the men
(D) flatter Lord Mayor's vanity
(E) get Lord Mayor to agree to the marriage of Lacy and Rose

30. What reason does the Earl of Lincoln give for his opposition to Lacy and Rose's marriage?

(A) Rose is not a pleasant person.
(B) Courtiers cannot marry.
(C) The wedding will be too expensive.
(D) Lacy does not love Rose.
(E) Lacy will not be able to provide for Rose.

GO ON TO THE NEXT PAGE →

31. The Earl of Lincoln's attitude toward his cousin can best be described as

    (A) censoriousness
    (B) apathy
    (C) affectation
    (D) dislike
    (E) affection

32. It can be inferred from the sentence "A goodly science for a gentleman/Of such descent!" (lines 32-33) that

    (A) the profession of shoemaker is not appropriate for someone of high birth
    (B) shoemakers often declare bankruptcy
    (C) the Earl of Lincoln admires the profession of shoemaker
    (D) as a shoemaker, the Earl of Lincoln's cousin will make a thousand pounds a year
    (E) shoemaking is a scientific occupation

33. Lord Mayor's attitude toward Lacy can best be described as

    (A) reluctant affection
    (B) avuncular indulgence
    (C) cautious approval
    (D) undeserved respect
    (E) disguised disapproval

34. The line "Well, fox, I understand your subtlety" (line 41)

    (A) allows Lord Mayor to speak to the Earl of Lincoln without others hearing them
    (B) entices the audience by revealing a secret
    (C) alienates the audience by prevarication
    (D) creates an atmosphere of unease in the play
    (E) insults the Earl of Lincoln

35. All of the following words are used to describe Lacy EXCEPT

    (A) "affected" (line 6)
    (B) "high" (line 12)
    (C) "unthrift" (line 19)
    (D) "jolly" (line 29)
    (E) "heir" (line 36)

36. This scene reveals a conflict between

    (A) generosity and frugality
    (B) prodigality and profligacy
    (C) youth and age
    (D) joy and melancholy
    (E) expression and emotions

37. The author has the Earl of Lincoln mention the French wars (line 52) in order to

    (A) reveal Lacy's new profession
    (B) foreshadow a military death
    (C) elucidate the causes of the conflict
    (D) explain a system of privilege
    (E) home in on a national debate

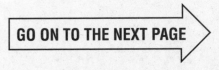

GO ON TO THE NEXT PAGE

Questions 38-45. **Read the following poem carefully before you choose your answers.**

"Fable"

In heaven
Some little blades of grass
Stood before God.
"What did you do?"
5 Then all save one of the little blades
Began eagerly to relate
The merits of their lives.
This one stayed a small way behind,
Ashamed.
10 Presently, God said,
"And what did you do?"
The little blade answered, "O my Lord,
Memory is bitter to me,
For if I did good deeds
15 I know not of them."
Then God, in all his splendor,
Arose from his throne.
"O best little blade of grass!" he said.

(1899)

38. It can be inferred that the speaker(s) in line 4 is/are

(A) an angel
(B) St. Peter
(C) the blades of grass
(D) God
(E) the one little blade of grass

39. God's attitude toward the little blade of grass may best be described as

(A) condescending
(B) neutral
(C) admiring
(D) disdainful
(E) morally superior

40. The main idea of the poem is that

(A) it is better to do nothing than too much
(B) it is better to forget if you have done something wrong
(C) it is better to be modest than to be boastful
(D) it is better to keep your problems to yourself
(E) if you need to tell your bad deeds to someone, you are not worthy of respect

GO ON TO THE NEXT PAGE

41. The word "presently" (line 10) means which of the following in the context of the poem?

   I. as a gift
   II. after a while
   III. changing the topic

   (A) I only
   (B) II only
   (C) I and III only
   (D) II and III only
   (E) I, II, and III

42. It can be inferred that the small blade was "ashamed" (line 9) because

   (A) it was smaller than the others
   (B) it was disgusted with the other blades of grass
   (C) it didn't feel worthy of God's attention
   (D) it was bitter and lonely
   (E) it thought its acts greater than the others' acts

43. The fact that God called the one blade "'O best'" (line 18) can best be characterized as

   (A) unexpected
   (B) satiric
   (C) tragic
   (D) comic
   (E) unfortunate

44. Which is the effect of lines 16-17 in relation to the rest of the poem?

   (A) They reveal God's egotism.
   (B) They heighten anticipation for the last line.
   (C) They shift the narrative voice.
   (D) They echo the last lines of the first stanza.
   (E) They reveal the poet's true feelings.

45. God's attitude toward the blades of grass as a group is

   (A) shameful
   (B) unstated
   (C) disgusted
   (D) disapproving
   (E) melancholy

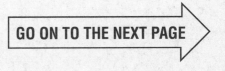

Questions 46-54. Read the following passage carefully before you choose your answers.

Everybody at all addicted to letter writing, without having much to say, which will include a large proportion of the female world at least, must feel with Lady Bertram, that she was out of luck in
5 having such a capital piece of Mansfield news, as the certainty of the Grants going to Bath, occur at a time when she could make no advantage of it, and will admit that it must have been very mortifying to her to see it fall to the share of their thankless
10 son, and treated as concisely possible at end of a long letter, instead of having it to spread over the largest part of a page of her own—For though Lady Bertram, rather at home in the epistolary line, having early in her marriage, from the want
15 of other employment, and the circumstance of Sir Thomas's being in Parliament, got into the way of making and keeping correspondents, and formed for herself a very creditable, commonplace, amplifying style, so that a very little matter was
20 enough for her; she could not do entirely without any; she must have something to write about, even to her niece, and being so soon to lose all the benefit of Dr. Grant's gouty symptoms and Mrs. Grant's morning calls, it was very hard upon her to
25 be deprived of one of the last epistolary uses she could put them to.
There was a rich amends, however, preparing for her. Lady Bertram's hour of good luck came. Within a few days from the receipt of
30 Edmund's letter, Fanny had one from her aunt, beginning thus:
"My dear Fanny,
I take up my pen to communicate some very alarming intelligence, which I make no doubt will
35 give you much concern."

(1814)

46. The narrative tone in the above piece can best be described as

(A) wry
(B) bitterly ironic
(C) detached
(D) melodramatic
(E) secretive

47. What is implied by the phrase "could make no advantage of it" (line 7) ?

(A) Lady Bertram could use the news to suit her best interest.
(B) Lady Bertram was unable to write about the news.
(C) Lady Bertram could not relay the news in a pleasant light.
(D) Lady Bertram could convey only part of the news.
(E) Lady Bertram was bound to secrecy.

48. In context, the word "want" (line 14) means

(A) requirement
(B) desire
(C) poverty
(D) lack
(E) defect

49. What is the "benefit" referred to in line 23 ?

(A) friends with whom to visit
(B) the ability to assist others
(C) a house full of visitors
(D) people willing to write letters
(E) news to write about

50. The "amplifying style" (line 19) is one in which

(A) things sound more important than they are
(B) small bits of news are stretched in importance
(C) the speaker's voice is very loud
(D) people are made to sound grand
(E) one writes in a large, bold print

GO ON TO THE NEXT PAGE

51. It can be inferred that Sir Thomas is

    (A) Lady Bertram's son
    (B) Lady Bertram's husband
    (C) a boarder at Mansfield
    (D) a relative of the Grants
    (E) a friend of Lady Bertram's

52. The last three lines serve to illustrate which of the following about Lady Bertram?

    (A) She has found something to write about.
    (B) She is spreading malicious rumors.
    (C) She is concerned about the news she is sending.
    (D) She is unaware of Fanny's feelings.
    (E) She is worried about her niece.

53. Lady Bertram is best described as

    (A) a social pariah
    (B) an unwanted family member
    (C) a disenfranchised member of society
    (D) a gossipy aristocrat
    (E) a disillusioned elderly woman

54. The phrase "even to her niece" (line 22) shows that Lady Bertram

    (A) doesn't much care for her niece
    (B) is unhappy with her niece
    (C) is uncomfortable around her niece
    (D) doesn't need to have much to say to her niece
    (E) dislikes the prospect of writing to her niece

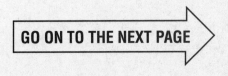

Questions 55-61. Read the following poem carefully before you choose your answers.

"Blue Girls"

Twirling your blue skirts, travelling the sward
Under the towers of your seminary,
Go listen to your teachers old and contrary
Without believing a word.

5   Tie the white fillets then about your hair
And think no more of what will come to pass
Than bluebirds that go walking on the grass
And chattering on the air.

Practice your beauty, blue girls, before it fail;
10   And I will cry with my loud lips and publish
Beauty which all our power shall never establish,
It is so frail.

For I could tell you a story which is true;
I know a woman with a terrible tongue,
15   Blear eyes fallen from blue,
All her perfections tarnished—yet it is not long
Since she was lovelier than any of you.

(1927)

55. The tone of the poem can best be described as

    (A) cautionary
    (B) mythic
    (C) sarcastic
    (D) optimistic
    (E) hopeful

56. The poem is primarily concerned with

    (A) the importance of beauty
    (B) the lesson to be learned from the past
    (C) the fleeting nature of youth
    (D) telling a story for the girls' benefit
    (E) the permanence of death

57. "Blear eyes fallen from blue" (line 15) is most probably meant to suggest that

    (A) the woman's beauty has deteriorated
    (B) the woman is tired
    (C) the woman is going blind
    (D) disease can happen suddenly
    (E) the girls are responsible for the woman's loss of beauty

GO ON TO THE NEXT PAGE

58. "And chattering on the air" (line 8) refers to

    I. the girls
    II. the bluebirds
    III. the teachers

(A) I only
(B) I and II only
(C) I and III only
(D) II and III only
(E) I, II, and III

59. The author's characterization of the woman in the last stanza can best be described as

(A) a description of decay
(B) unyielding and hurtful
(C) disdainful and disgusted
(D) pleasant and nostalgic
(E) full of unhidden emotion

60. The phrases "Without believing a word" (line 4) and "think no more" (line 6) illustrate the girls'

(A) innate sense of suspicion
(B) inherent difficulty with understanding subjects
(C) lack of concern about weighty subjects
(D) frail nature
(E) disregard for the feelings of others

61. The poem's theme could best be described as

(A) she who hesitates is lost
(B) beauty is a fading flower
(C) all that glitters is not gold
(D) beauty is truth, truth beauty
(E) a penny saved is a penny earned

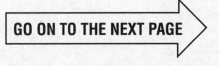

GO ON TO THE NEXT PAGE

How to Score The Princeton Review
Practice SAT Literature Subject Test

When you take the real exam, the proctors will collect your test booklet and bubble sheet and send your answer sheet to New Jersey where a computer looks at the pattern of filled-in ovals on your answer sheet and gives you a score. We couldn't include even a small computer with this book, so we are providing this more primitive way of scoring your exam.

Determining Your Score

STEP 1 Using the answer key on the next page, determine how many questions you got right and how many you got wrong on the test. Remember, questions that you do not answer do not count as either right or wrong answers.

STEP 2 List the number of right answers here.

(A) _____

STEP 3 List the number of wrong answers here. Now divide that number by 4. (Use a calculator if you're feeling particularly lazy.)

(B) _____ ÷ 4 = (C) _____

STEP 4 Subtract the number of wrong answers divided by 4 from the number of correct answers. Round this score to the nearest whole number. This is your raw score.

(A) – (C) = _____

STEP 5 To determine your real score, take the number from Step 4 and look it up in the left-hand column of the Score Conversion Table on page 146; the corresponding score on the right is your score on the exam.

Answer Key to Practice SAT Literature Subject Test 1

1. B	16. A	31. A	46. A
2. C	17. B	32. A	47. B
3. B	18. B	33. E	48. D
4. E	19. C	34. B	49. E
5. E	20. E	35. E	50. B
6. C	21. D	36. E	51. B
7. A	22. B	37. A	52. A
8. D	23. C	38. D	53. D
9. E	24. A	39. C	54. D
10. D	25. D	40. C	55. A
11. C	26. B	41. B	56. C
12. C	27. A	42. C	57. A
13. A	28. B	43. A	58. B
14. D	29. C	44. B	59. A
15. B	30. E	45. B	60. C
			61. B

SAT Literature Subject Test—Score Conversion Table

Raw Score	College Board Scaled Score	Raw Score	College Board Scaled Score
61	800	25	520
60	800	24	510
59	800	23	500
58	800	22	490
57	800	21	490
56	800	20	480
55	790	19	470
54	780	18	460
53	780	17	450
52	770	16	440
51	760	15	430
50	750	14	4120
49	740	13	410
48	730	12	410
47	720	11	400
46	710	10	390
45	700	09	380
44	700	08	370
43	690	07	360
42	680	06	350
41	670	05	350
40	660	04	340
39	650	03	330
38	640	02	320
37	630	01	310
36	620	00	300
35	620	−01	300
34	610	−02	290
33	600	−03	280
32	590	−04	270
31	580	−05	260
30	570	−06	250
29	560	−07	240
28	550	−08	240
27	540	−09	230
26	530	−10	220
		−11	210
		−12	200
		−13	200
		−14	200
		−15	200

Chapter 14
Practice Test 1:
Answers and Explanations

Answers and Explanations

Question	Answer	Explanation
1	B	This is a good example of a "least worst" answer. There is no labor involved (A). All we see Babette do is "dance" (line 13), so life is not very "difficult" (C). Nature is not "enigmatic" (a mystery) (D). The differences between Maman-Nainaine and Babette can hardly be called a "battle." So by Process of Elimination, the answer must be (B).
2	C	Choice (C) is the best answer, because Maman-Nainaine says Babette's visit depends on the figs, which has nothing to do with the visit. So she must have her own reasons for linking the two—"her own logic." Babette wants to visit her cousins, so the situation is hardly "serious" (A). She may be "overly strict," but we don't have enough information to affirm that (B). Choice (D) cannot be the answer because there is no "punishment." And nothing suggests that "figs were her favorite fruit" (E).
3	B	Choice (B) is the answer because Maman-Nainaine wants Babette to wait to make the visit, but Babette wants to go right now. Maman-Nainaine is patient; Babette is not. Nothing in the passage proves that Maman-Nainaine's judgment is bad (A). In lines 1–8, the figs have not ripened yet, so there is no passage of time (C). Babette does not talk back to Maman-Nainaine, so there is no insolence (D) or argument (E).
4	E	Maman-Nainaine is patient (line 10) (E). Maman-Nainaine does not look down on Babette, so she is not "contemptuous" (A). Nothing she says to Babette is "flippant" (B). She does not give in to Babette's wishes, so she is not "reluctantly accepting" (C). There is neither joy nor optimism in the passage (D).
5	E	"Ripe" and "bloom" both refer to later stages of life—they refer to Maman-Nainaine, not Babette, so the answer is (E). It is true that Maman-Nainaine is "patient" and Babette is "restless," so (A) is not the answer. Babette is young; she wants to make the visit "early," while Maman-Nainaine is "late" in life (B). The unripe figs represent Babette—they are "green," while Maman-Nainaine is like a ripe fig—"purple" (C). Maman-Nainaine is older—she "sat" while Babette is young and "danced" (D). (Note: Remember to circle "EXCEPT" and mark each answer with a "Y" for "yes" or an "N" for "no" to find the odd man out.)
6	C	Just as the figs are a symbol of Babette's maturity, so are the chrysanthemums symbolic (C). It is not illogical of Maman-Nainaine to mention chrysanthemums, as the story shows she measures time by the flowering of nature (A). There is nothing ironic about the statement (B). Literature is not referenced (D). The sentence does not advance the story beyond the boundaries of Maman-Nainaine's and Babette's relationship (E).
7	A	By taking time to peel the figs, Maman-Nainaine is making sure they're ripe (A). There is no cooking in the story (B), nor is superstition the reason for Maman-Nainaine's behavior (C). Although she may be refined, the action is not the illustration of refinement (D). We don't see Maman-Nainaine mock Babette (E).

Question	Answer	Explanation
8	D	The two women are different, yet nature forges on, so (D) is the correct answer. In the context of the sentence the word "though" does not show disagreement (A). No moral is given (B). There is no evidence that the figs were not important (C). Babette is restless, not annoyed (E).
9	E	The narration is that of an impartial observer (E). It is not disapproving (A), nor is it first person (B). The protagonist (either Maman-Nainaine or Babette) does not narrate the story (C), nor do we have any evidence that this narrator is unreliable (D).
10	D	Who's Jove? Who cares! This is obviously a reference to someone, so the word "allusion" is our best bet (D). There is no "play on words" (A), nor any "contradiction" (B). Although the poem might be fanciful, there is no "hyperbole" (exaggeration) (C). There are no underlying symbols, so the poem is not an "allegory" (E).
11	C	He thinks he sees his wife as a ghost, like Jove's son gave the image of a ghost to Alcestis's husband, so the line refers to both "my late espoused Saint" (the narrator's wife) (Statement I) and to Alcestis (Statement II). The "glad husband" is not the one "rescued from death" (Statement III).
12	C	The poem says that the wife was purified and that the poet plans to see her in heaven, so "save" means "deliver from sin and punishment" (C). Because she is dead, she is not preserved (A), nor is she kept in health (B). She is neither rescued from harm (D) nor maintained (E)—don't fall into the trap answer just because the definition of "save" is "maintained."
13	A	When the poet wakes up, the ghost image is gone, and although it is day, he feels like it's night (A). Although the narrator feels grief, there is no evidence that he is depressed (B). This is nothing like a sonnet (C), nor does it parallel any construction (D). The fact that although it is day when he wakes he feels like it's night does not suggest optimism (E).
14	D	He is asleep and sees a ghost, so it is reasonable to infer that he is "dreaming" (D). There is nothing in the poem to suggest that she did not have these qualities in life (A). The fact that he knows it is "fancied" suggests that he knows he is dreaming (B). He is dreaming, so there is nothing capricious about the image, which comes to him unbidden (C), and he realizes it is a dream, so he is not delusional (E).
15	B	He clearly loves his wife a great deal, so he is "reverential" (B). He may be "inconsolable," but not in his attitude toward his wife (A). Again, she is dead, so he does not have a "hopeful" attitude toward her (C). Neither "incongruous" (bizarre) (D) nor "obsequious" (fawning) (E) makes sense in this context.
16	A	The poem is about how he misses his wife, so (A) is the correct answer. There is nothing to suggest the poet is struggling with death (B), nor does he lament that death is unjust (C) (although you may think so, it's not in the poem). It's more about the poet himself than it is about what happens to the body/soul, so it's not about immortality (D), and the main point is not a belief in heaven (E).

Question	Answer	Explanation
17	B	The three "g" words in the surrounding lines are good examples of alliteration (B). "Glad" does not mean overwhelmed (A), nor does it stress the individuality of the husband (C). "Glad" does not help distinguish between Jove's son and the husband (D), and the narrator is not glad in line 1 (E).
18	B	The day (and the light of his wife) contrasts with the night that the narrator feels (B). The wife was inclining (leaning) over to embrace the narrator when he awoke, so these are not opposites (A). "Full sight" and "without restraint" mean the same thing (C), as do "wash't" and "purification" (D). "Sight" and "shin'd" don't have a relationship (E).
19	C	Mr. Keeble is stuttering because he is afraid of his wife (C). There is no evidence that he is a "feeble man" (A), just that he is afraid of his wife. Disjointed speech (B) is an aftereffect; the cause is his fear. It does not serve to slow the conversation (D). It does not elucidate (explain, shed light on) the main point; in fact, it obfuscates it (hides, makes more confusing) (E).
20	E	A mythological allusion refers to something—usually a work of literature in the myth genre. Pygmalion and Galatea are characters in mythology (E). Lines 28–29 do not refer to anything (A), nor do lines 20–21 (B). In lines 17–18 the narrator is exaggerating but not referring to myth (C), while (D) refers to a place, not a work of literature.
21	D	Breathing is the only one of these examples that is a normal human characteristic, so (D) is the answer. Answer (A) compares her to a liquid that has turned solid, while (B) compares her to a statue. Choice (C) continues the statue comparison, while (E) suggests that the word "Lincolnshire" is "like some spell" (simile).
22	B	Answer choice (B) is a figure of speech meaning that the farm is making lots of money, which is why Mr. Keeble wants to invest in it. There is nothing to suggest the farm is doing something illegal (A). The investment may or may not be unnecessary, but that has nothing to do with "coining money" (C). Answer choice (D) takes the turn of phrase too literally. The farm is in Lincolnshire, but there is nothing to suggest that Lincolnshire itself is a good way to make money (E).
23	C	Mrs. Keeble reacts "icily" before Mr. Keeble can even explain—so she is opposed to the idea (C). She is not amused (A), nor is she disgusted (B). She obviously cares, so she is not apathetic (D), and she is icy, so she is not neutral (E).
24	A	Mr. Keeble is fiddling nervously while he talks, so all of the examples are physical illustrations of fidgeting except "keenly alive," which simply means he's aware (A). He rattles keys nervously (B) and (D), and doesn't look at his wife (C) and (E), because he thinks he knows how she'll react.

Question	Answer	Explanation
25	D	Mr. Keeble has put a lot of thought into this, so he must be pretending he isn't sure of the location in an attempt to make it appear as an afterthought or to de-emphasize it (D). He obviously knows where it is (A), and if he didn't think the location was important, he wouldn't have mentioned it (B). There is no evidence that he is forgetting (C), and if he had wanted to conceal the location, he would not have said it (E).
26	B	He is obviously intimidated by his wife—he is afraid of her (Statement III), but there is no evidence that he needs her approval—we don't know his motives for telling her about the farm (Statement I), nor is there any evidence that she disgusts him (Statement II).
27	A	Because she asks the question icily, we can infer that she is not excited about the idea of lending money (A). She is not interested in the proposition (B), and we know nothing of Mr. Keeble's mission (C). She is icy, so she is not keeping an open mind (D), nor is she curious (E).
28	B	Lord Mayor has invited the Earl of Lincoln to dinner several times; therefore, "numerous" is the best answer (B). "Groceries" (A) is a too-literal synonym for "sundries," as is "provisions" (C). There have been many dinners, so "infrequent" (D) is not correct, nor is "few" (E).
29	C	The scene is about how Lord Mayor and his daughter are of a different social class than the Earl of Lincoln, so (C) is the best answer. The Earl of Lincoln does not plan to return Lord Mayor's generosity: "Seldom or never can we be so kind/To make requital of your courtesy" (lines 3–4) (A). Although he does acknowledge Lord Mayor's magnanimity, this is not the main effect of the lines (B). The phrase is not designed to flatter (D). Neither of the men wants the younger generation to marry (E).
30	E	The Earl of Lincoln says that Lacy spends too much money, so he won't be able to provide for Rose (E). By saying Rose is "mean," Lord Mayor means that she is of a lower class, not that she isn't nice (A). There is no evidence that courtiers cannot marry (B). No mention is made of the cost of a wedding (C). Lacy *does* love Rose: "He is much affected" (line 6) (D).
31	A	The Earl of Lincoln does not approve of his cousin's spendthrift ways (A). He is not apathetic, because he obviously cares about his cousin's welfare (B). "Affectation," in this context, means "in love" (C). He does not necessarily "dislike" his cousin (D). "Affection" is not the Earl of Lincoln's primary emotion, as he insults Lacy (E).
32	A	The Earl of Lincoln does not approve of Lacy's new profession—the line is sarcastic (A). There is nothing that tells us how much shoemakers earn, (B) and (D). The Earl of Lincoln does not want his cousin to be a shoemaker, so he obviously does not admire the profession (C). Shoemaking is not a scientific occupation (E).

Question	Answer	Explanation
33	E	Lord Mayor claims his daughter is too common for Lacy, but his aside shows that he does not think that Lacy is a good match: "I scorn to call him son-in-law" (line 46), although he does not admit this (E). He doesn't feel affection (A), nor does he feel like an uncle (avuncular) (B). He never approves the match (C), nor is there any evidence that he respects Lacy (D).
34	B	An "aside" is when a character speaks directly to the audience while the action "freezes." The audience is intrigued because it is revealed that the Earl of Lincoln is up to no good (B). The aside is designed so that other characters cannot hear it (A). The audience is not alienated by the aside (why would a playwright want to alienate an audience?) (C). No atmosphere of unease is created (D), and because the Earl of Lincoln can't hear the aside, it is not designed to insult him (E).
35	E	Lacy is never described as an "heir," although Rose is (E). Lacy is described as "affected" (line 6) (A), "high" (line 12) (B), "unthrift" (line 19) (C), and "jolly" (line 29) (D).
36	E	Neither of the characters is saying what he is thinking—as revealed by the asides (E). No one is described as frugal (A). Prodigious means "large"—there is no mention of size (B). There is no conflict between the younger and older generations (C). There is no contrast between happiness and sorrow in this passage (D).
37	A	The Earl of Lincoln most likely mentions the wars because Lacy has just been appointed a soldier (A). We can't know if there will be a death (B). The Earl does not explain why they are fighting the French (C). The lines do not explain the class system in place (D). There is no mention of a national debate (E).
38	D	The blades of grass are standing before God, so presumably God is talking to them (D). There is no angel (A), nor is St. Peter in the poem (B). God is asking the blades to justify their entry into heaven, so God—not the blades of grass—is speaking (E).
39	C	God is happy at the one little blade's comments so (C) is the best answer. God is not "condescending" (A), "neutral" (B), or "disdainful" (D). God does not show that He is "morally superior" in this poem (E).
40	C	God rewards the one little blade of grass for his modesty in contrast with the other blades' boastfulness (C). There is no evidence that it is better to do nothing (A). The blade is not rewarded for his forgetfulness (B). The blades are boasting of their accomplishments, not their problems (D). There is no mention of having to tell your bad deeds to someone (E).
41	B	The word "presently" means "after a while." It has nothing to do with presents or gifts, nor does it mean that the speaker is changing the topic.

Question	Answer	Explanation
42	C	The other blades were all boasting, so the one little one is ashamed and hanging back because he does not feel worthy (C). All of the blades of grass were little; their heights are not compared (A). There is no evidence of disgust (B), or bitterness or loneliness (D). Answer (E) is incorrect because the blade thought his acts were less worthy than the others, not more worthy.
43	A	God's declaration that the one little blade is the best is surprising ("unexpected") because it was the one blade that did not admit to any accomplishments (A). There is nothing "satiric" (making fun of) about the phrase (B). It is neither "tragic" (C) nor "comic" (D), nor, since the blade is probably headed to heaven, is there anything "unfortunate" (E).
44	B	God rising up is a dramatic pause which heightens the suspense of the poem (B). There is no evidence that God is egotistical (A), nor is there a shift or change in how the narrator sounds (C). These lines do not echo anything in the poem (and it's hard to tell if there is more than one stanza) (D). We cannot know the poet's true feelings (E).
45	B	We do not hear about how God reacts to the other little blades of grass, so His attitude can best be described as "unstated" (B). God is not "shameful" (A), nor is He "disgusted" (C) or "disapproving" (D). He is not "melancholy" (sad) (E).
46	A	The narrator is poking fun at Lady Bertram so that the reader will laugh, so the tone can best be described as "wry" (A). There is no bitterness in the passage (B). The narrator is fairly closely involved in the story, so "detached" is not correct (C). Although Lady Bertram herself is "melodramatic," the narrator is not (D). And the narrator is free with her opinions and words, so "secretive" is not correct (E).
47	B	Lady Bertram likes to write about gossip. She can't write about this news (because the son already has), so it is of no use to her (B). Lady Bertram could not use the news (A). There is nothing that suggests Lady Bertram would relay the news unpleasantly (C). There is no evidence that she could write about only part of the news (D), nor are we told that she was bound to secrecy (E).
48	D	"The want of other employment" means she lacked anything else to do, so (D) is the best answer. She did not require other employment (A). "Desire" (B) is a trap answer because it is a common synonym for "want." There is no mention of finances (C), and we are not told that her employment is defective (E).
49	E	The Grants are going away, so Lady Bertram won't be able to write about Mr. Grant's illness or things that Mrs. Grant says when she comes over, i.e., she'll have no news (E). There is no evidence that she enjoys the Grants, except for the gossip they provide (A), and she does not assist them (B). There is no evidence that her house is full, nor that they stay with her (C). She has many correspondents (D).

Question	Answer	Explanation
50	B	The phrase is explained in the text that follows it: "so that a very little matter was enough for her" meaning that she could make inconsequential news important (B). She does not inflate the importance of things (A). Answer choice (C) is a too-literal synonym of "amplifying." There is no evidence that she tries to make people sound more important than they are (D), nor is there any mention of her penmanship (E).
51	B	Sir Thomas must be Lady Bertram's husband because she is left with nothing to do when he is in Parliament (plus, if she is a lady, then he must be a lord). There is no evidence that he is her son (A), nor that he is a border (C), nor that he is at all connected to the Grants (D), and his Parliament attendance affects her too much for him to be just a mere friend (E).
52	A	At the end of the passage, Lady Bertram writes to Fanny, so she must have something to say (A). We don't know what the news is, so we cannot say it is "malicious" (mean) (B). She is not concerned about the news, but rather predicts that Fanny will feel concerned (C), so she is aware of Fanny's feelings (D). If she were really worried about her niece, why would she be telling her the news (E)?
53	D	Lady Bertram likes to gossip, and she is a woman of leisure and title (D). She has friends; she is not a "social pariah" (A). We don't know what others in her family think of her (B). She seems to be very connected to society (C), and we don't know anything about her age, except that she has a niece (which says little about how old she is) (E).
54	D	The phrase implies that she needs the least amount of news to write her niece, but doesn't even have that (D). We have no evidence that she doesn't like her niece (she is obviously close to her) (A), or that she is mad at (B) or uncomfortable around (C) her niece. Lady Bertram loves writing letters to anyone, so (E) is not correct.
55	A	The poem is a warning to young women about the pitfalls of vanity (A). There are no myths in the poem (B). The poet is not "sarcastic" (C). The poet warns of fading beauty, so the poet is neither "optimistic" (D) nor "hopeful" (E). Think, because "optimistic" and "hopeful" are synonyms, they can't both be the right answer, so they should both be eliminated.
56	C	The poem is a warning to young women that beauty fades (C). There is no discussion of the importance of beauty (A). There is no "past lesson" to be learned (B). The primary purpose is not to tell a particular story (D). There is no discussion of death (E).

Question	Answer	Explanation
57	A	The last two lines of the poem describe the woman as someone who used to be pretty and is now old and ugly, of which her eyes are an example (A). There is no evidence that the woman is tired (B). That she is blind is a too-literal interpretation of the line (C). There is no mention of disease, only old age (D). Girls cannot be responsible for someone's loss of beauty (E).
58	B	The vain girls are compared to bluebirds—the two groups chatter among themselves (Statements I and II). The teachers are not the carefree chatterers that the poem mentions (Statement III).
59	A	The author describes a beautiful woman who got ugly with age, so (A) is the best answer. The author is not unyielding (stubborn) (B). There is no evidence of the author's disgust (C). The memories are not particularly "pleasant": ("terrible," "tarnished") (D). The emotions are not hidden (E).
60	C	The girls don't listen to their teachers because the teachers are old, and they don't worry about the future ("weighty subjects") (C). There is no sense of suspicion (A) or the notion that subjects are hard to understand (B). They are not described as frail (in fact, they "twirl" their skirts) (D). There is no evidence that they disregard others' feelings (E).
61	B	The theme of the poem is that people should not waste time on vanity because it does not last (B). Acting quickly is not a theme (A). Neither are the trappings of wealth (C). Truth (D) is not a theme, nor is frugality (E).

Chapter 15
Practice Test 2

PRACTICE SAT LITERATURE
SUBJECT TEST 2

TEST 2

Your responses to the SAT Literature Subject Test questions should
be filled in on Test 2 of your answer sheet.

LITERATURE TEST 2

Directions: This test consists of selections from literary works and questions on their content, form, and style. After reading each passage or poem, choose the best answer to each question and fill in the corresponding oval on the answer sheet.

Note: Pay particular attention to questions that contain the words NOT, LEAST, or EXCEPT.

Questions 1-9. Read the following poem carefully before you choose your answers.

"Promises Like Pie-Crust"

Promise me no promises,
   So will I not promise you:
Keep we both our liberties,
   Never false and never true:
5 Let us hold the die uncast,
   Free to come as free to go:
For I cannot know your past,
   And of mine what can you know?

You, so warm, may once have been
10   Warmer towards another one:
I, so cold, may once have seen
   Sunlight, once have felt the sun:
Who shall show us if it was
   Thus indeed in time of old?
15 Fades the image from the glass,
   And the fortune is not told.

If you promised, you might grieve
   For lost liberty again:
If I promised, I believe
20   I should fret to break the chain.
Let us be the friends we were,
   Nothing more but nothing less:
Many thrive on frugal fare
   Who would perish of excess.

(1861)

1. The promises referred to in the poem are

(A) pledges to share one another's innermost secrets
(B) articles of incorporation
(C) items in a prenuptial agreement
(D) resolution never to see one another again
(E) marriage vows

GO ON TO THE NEXT PAGE ⇨

2. In the second stanza, the speaker reveals that

    (A) she yearns for the love of someone who is oblivious to her
    (B) her listener has expressed more ardent sentiments toward her than she has expressed toward him
    (C) the listener does not reciprocate her feelings
    (D) she is incapable of deep emotional attachment
    (E) she is heartbroken over the end of a previous relationship

3. The speaker compares her current relationship with the person to whom the poem is addressed to

    (A) one between strangers
    (B) a roll of the dice
    (C) one governed by reciprocal obligations
    (D) a restrained diet of plain food
    (E) an image in a crystal ball

4. "Sunlight" (line 12) is used as a symbol for

    (A) innocence
    (B) genuine mutual love
    (C) purity
    (D) absolute confidence in the rightness of a decision
    (E) perfect understanding

5. Which of the following is NOT implied in the poem as a reason to avoid entering into promises?

    (A) One person can never fully know another.
    (B) A promise can be broken without the person to whom the promise was made ever knowing.
    (C) To make a promise denies one of a degree of personal liberty.
    (D) One cannot be judged faithful or unfaithful to a commitment that has not been promised.
    (E) One can never fully know the situations or feelings of those who made successful and binding promises in the past.

6. In context, "fret" (line 20) most nearly means

    (A) irritate
    (B) chafe
    (C) agitate
    (D) worry
    (E) corrode

7. Which of the following best expresses the meaning of the last two lines of the poem?

    (A) Some people are not meant to enjoy the richness of life, just as some cannot digest rich food.
    (B) When it comes to relationships, something is better than nothing.
    (C) For some people, the potential of happiness is more satisfying than the reality of happiness because the potential cannot be diminished over time.
    (D) Not every relationship is worth the risk entailed to the participants.
    (E) Some relationships are better when they are not too serious.

8. The tone of the poem as a whole can best be described as

    (A) delicate but firm
    (B) disappointed but unapologetic
    (C) ambivalent but patronizing
    (D) world-weary and vague
    (E) harsh and unyielding

9. The simile of the title is apt because

    (A) both promises and pie-crust are sweet
    (B) both promises and pie-crust are meant to be filled
    (C) both promises and pie-crust are easily broken
    (D) the speaker has overindulged in rich food
    (E) the speaker denies herself all pleasures in life

GO ON TO THE NEXT PAGE

Questions 10-17. Read the following passage carefully before you choose your answers.

Studies serve for delight, for ornament, and for ability. Their chief use for delight is in privateness and retiring; for ornament, is in discourse; and for ability, is in the judgment and
5 disposition of business. For expert men can execute, and perhaps judge of particulars, one by one; but the general counsels, and the plots and marshalling of affairs come best from those that are learned. To spend too much time in studies
10 is sloth; to use them too much for ornament is affectation; to make judgment wholly by their rules is the humor of a scholar. They perfect nature, and are perfected by experience: for natural abilities are like natural plants, that need
15 pruning by study; and studies themselves do give forth directions too much at large, except they be bounded in by experience. Crafty men contemn* studies, simple men admire them, and wise men use them; for they teach not their own
20 use; but that is a wisdom without them and above them, won by observation. Read not to contradict and confute, nor to believe and take for granted, nor to find talk and discourse, but to weigh and consider.

(c. 1597)

*have contempt for

10. The author's primary purpose is to

(A) demonstrate a display of learned eloquence
(B) encourage pupils to study diligently
(C) discuss the proper means to education
(D) distinguish the more serious from the less dignified motives for study
(E) dissuade students from applying their learning to unethical pursuits

11. By "expert men" (line 5) the author most nearly means

(A) persons with competence in specific activities, but who lack general education
(B) persons who have mastered a craft or trade
(C) persons who carry out the decisions of others
(D) persons who have devoted themselves to their studies
(E) persons who conduct the concrete business of the day

12. The author compares "abilities" and "plants" (line 14) to make the point that

(A) individuals must discipline themselves as they grow to maturity
(B) some students learn profusely while others learn little or slowly
(C) individuals must be nurtured and protected as growing plants must be
(D) education encourages individuals to develop in conformity with one another
(E) education shapes and refines an individual's innate qualities

13. Which of the following cautions is NOT conveyed in the passage?

(A) The organization of large undertakings is best left to persons who have read widely and deeply.
(B) It is possible to be overzealous in the pursuit of knowledge.
(C) One should not flaunt one's learning ostentatiously.
(D) Scholars should live in strict accordance with precepts gained through their study.
(E) The knowledge gained from books must be tested against one's firsthand experience in the world.

14. With which of the following words or phrases could "admire" (line 18) be replaced without changing the meaning of the sentence?

    (A) are awed by
    (B) profess to respect
    (C) enjoy
    (D) are envious of
    (E) are naturally drawn toward

15. Which of these stylistic devices is most prominent in the author's prose?

    (A) elaborate metaphor
    (B) hyperbole
    (C) neatly balanced syntactic oppositions
    (D) alliteration
    (E) long, convoluted sentences

16. Reading, according to the author, is above all else a source for one's

    (A) controversial opinions
    (B) moral and religious beliefs
    (C) quiet amusement
    (D) stimulating conversation
    (E) private deliberation

17. The tone of the passage can best be described as

    (A) pious
    (B) didactic
    (C) satiric
    (D) moralistic
    (E) contentious

GO ON TO THE NEXT PAGE

Questions 18-24. Read the following poem carefully before you choose your answers.

"The Errand"

"On you go now! Run, son, like the devil
And tell your mother to try
To find me a bubble for the spirit level
And a new knot for this tie."

5   But still he was glad, I know, when I stood my ground,
Putting it up to him
With a smile that trumped his smile and his fool's errand,
Waiting for the next move in the game.

(1996)

18. The theme of the poem concerns

(A) rites of passage that mark the beginning of
    adolescence
(B) the contest of wills between one generation
    and the next
(C) the futility of needless chores with which
    parents occupy their children
(D) a boy's developing relationship with his father
    as the boy matures
(E) the resentment that lingers in the poet's
    memory about childhood

19. The errand described in the poem is a quest for

(A) nonsensical components that do not form a
    coherent whole
(B) tools the speaker needs to continue his work
(C) someone in the neighborhood more foolish
    than the man's son
(D) degrees of understanding that come with
    maturity
(E) common ground on which father and son can
    identify with each other

20. Which of the following distinctions does NOT
    characterize the difference between the two
    stanzas?

(A) a shift from perfect rhyme to slant rhyme
(B) a change in speaker
(C) the passage of time
(D) a movement from metaphorical to literal
    language
(E) a switch from remembered speech to
    reflection

21. Which of the following is implied by the poet's
    use of the word "still" (line 5) ?

(A) The father's jovial spirits were not ultimately
    dampened when his son did not assume the
    errand.
(B) The father's pleased response to his son's
    refusal will continue indefinitely.
(C) The game between the father and son will
    continue indefinitely.
(D) The father did not express his gladness to his
    son.
(E) The boy's father was disappointed when his
    son did not assume the errand.

GO ON TO THE NEXT PAGE

22. Which of the following is nearest in meaning to "Putting it up to him" (line 6) ?

    (A) demonstrating to him the poet's awareness of his joke
    (B) challenging him to find a bubble for himself
    (C) refusing defiantly to honor his request
    (D) handing up to him the items he had asked for
    (E) turning the joke back around on him

23. "Trumped" (line 7) is an allusion to

    (A) a dramatic fanfare announcing an arrival or significant development
    (B) a winning play in a game of cards
    (C) showy but worthless finery
    (D) a squashing sound under one's feet
    (E) the eclipse of one source of light by a brighter source

24. In the last line the poet suggests that

    (A) the father will send his son on another, more serious errand
    (B) the father's goal is to make his son appear ridiculous
    (C) the father's response to his son's recognition will be significantly delayed
    (D) the father will continue to good-humoredly tease and test his son
    (E) the father and son will always engage in prankish contests

GO ON TO THE NEXT PAGE

Questions 25-33. Read the following passage carefully before you choose your answers.

Joe's funeral was the finest thing Orange
County had ever seen with Negro eyes. The
motor hearse, the Cadillac and Buick carriages;
Dr. Henderson there in his Lincoln; the hosts
5 from far and wide. Then again the gold and
red and purple, the gloat and glamor of the
secret orders, each with its insinuations of
power and glory undreamed of by the
uninitiated. People on farm horses and mules;
10 babies riding astride of brothers' and sisters'
backs. The Elks band ranked at the church
door and playing "Safe in the Arms of Jesus"
with such a dominant drum rhythm that it could
be stepped off smartly by the long line as it
15 filed inside. The Little Emperor of the cross-
roads was leaving Orange County as he had
come—with the out-stretched hand of power.
Janie starched and ironed her face and came
set in the funeral behind her veil. It was like a
20 wall of stone and steel. The funeral was going
on outside. All things concerning death and
burial were said and done. Finish. End.
Nevermore. Darkness. Deep hole.
Dissolution. Eternity. Weeping and wailing
25 outside. Inside the expensive black folds were
resurrection and life. She did not reach outside
for anything, nor did the things of death reach
inside to disturb her calm. She sent her face to
Joe's funeral, and herself went rollicking with
30 the springtime across the world. After a while
the people finished their celebration and Janie
went on home.

(1937)

25. Which of the following is the closest paraphrase of
the first sentence of the passage?

(A) Joe's funeral was the finest display the black
people of Orange County had ever seen.
(B) Joe's funeral was the finest display of black
people that the white people of Orange
County had ever seen.
(C) The finest-looking black people in Orange
County were all in evidence at Joe's funeral.
(D) The ceremony of Joe's funeral was not much
compared to an average funeral for a white
person in Orange County.
(E) Joe's funeral gave the white people in
attendance a chance to experience the world
from a black point of view.

26. The effect of the first paragraph is to

(A) contrast the pomp and display of the
assembled mourners with Janie's genuine
grief
(B) show how Joe's funeral was not in keeping
with the tendencies of his life
(C) demonstrate the importance with which Joe
was viewed in his community
(D) illustrate the fruitless nature of our attempts to
disguise the starkness of death.
(E) emphasize the ephemerality of life

27. It can be inferred that the mourners at Joe's funeral

(A) are deeply grieved by Joe's death
(B) are exaggerating their respect for Joe out of
sympathy for Janie
(C) are insincerely using Joe's funeral as an
excuse for a flamboyant celebration
(D) are all members of a single, tight-knit
community
(E) would be surprised to learn of Janie's sense of
detachment from the proceedings

28. "Secret orders" (line 7) most probably refers to

(A) the self-importance felt by those driving
expensive automobiles to the funeral
(B) the silent commands governing the conduct of
some attendees at the funeral
(C) members of fraternal organizations who came
to the funeral dressed in their clubs' regalia
(D) the haughty behavior of people attending the
funeral whom the other attendees had never
met or seen
(E) the majestic, heavenly hosts of which Joe is
now presumably a member

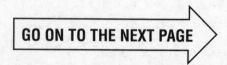

GO ON TO THE NEXT PAGE

29. Why is Janie's veil described as "a wall of stone and steel" (lines 19-20) ?

   (A) The veil allows Janie to suppress her anguish and maintain her composure during the funeral.
   (B) The veil screens Janie from the accusing stares of the mourners at the funeral.
   (C) The veil represents the solidity of Janie's emotional state.
   (D) The veil allows Janie to endure the formal pretense of mourning at Joe's funeral, which is not in keeping with her true feelings.
   (E) The veil allows Janie to hide her true feelings from herself until after the funeral.

30. What is the effect of the phrase "the people finished their celebration" (line 31) ?

   (A) It draws attention to the funeral's emphasis on the virtues of Joe's life and achievements.
   (B) It emphasizes the communal nature of the funeral, which brings together individuals from all ranks of society.
   (C) It emphasizes Janie's isolation from the others at the funeral.
   (D) It emphasizes the distances from which people had traveled to attend the funeral.
   (E) It points out that celebrations are by nature temporary and must give way to the routines of daily life.

31. The style of the passage is characterized by the repeated use of

   (A) African American dialect
   (B) grammatically incomplete sentences
   (C) religious imagery
   (D) ironic turns of phrase
   (E) oxymoron

32. Which of the following phrases from the passage best expresses Janie's emotional state during the funeral?

   (A) "gloat and glamor" (line 6)
   (B) "starched and ironed" (line 18)
   (C) "Darkness. Deep hole." (line 23)
   (D) "Weeping and wailing" (line 24)
   (E) "resurrection and life" (line 26)

33. Which of the following inferences can be made about Janie's relationship to Joe?

   (A) Janie knew Joe only as a casual acquaintance and is unmoved by his death.
   (B) Janie cared deeply for Joe and has not yet fully experienced the shock of his death.
   (C) Janie felt a strong dislike for Joe and must disguise her antipathy at his funeral.
   (D) Janie's relationship with Joe was such that she feels unburdened and revitalized by his death.
   (E) Janie's feelings for Joe were a secret to the community and must be suppressed at his funeral.

GO ON TO THE NEXT PAGE

Questions 34-42. Read the following poem carefully before you choose your answers.

"The Mower to the Glowworms"

Ye living lamps, by whose dear light
The nightingale does sit so late,
And studying all the summer night,
Her matchless songs does meditate;

5   Ye country comets, that portend
No war nor prince's funeral,
Shining unto no higher end
Than to presage the grass's fall;

Ye glowworms, whose officious flame
10   To wandering mowers shows the way,
That in the night have lost their aim,
And after foolish fires do stray;

Your courteous lights in vain you waste,
Since Juliana here is come,
15   For she my mind hath so displaced
That I shall never find my home.

(c. 1650)

34. The speaker of the poem first addresses the glowworms by epithets that draw attention to the insects' natural

   (A) intelligence
   (B) tranquility
   (C) luminosity
   (D) inconsequence
   (E) mortality

35. The speaker of the poem describes glowworms as providing assistance to

   I. nightingales
   II. princes
   III. mowers

   (A) I only
   (B) II only
   (C) III only
   (D) I and III only
   (E) I, II, and III

36. In its context, the word "portend" (line 5) means

   (A) "predict," and alludes to the superstition that the motion of glowworms could be interpreted to foretell future events
   (B) "predict," and alludes to the superstition that comets, meteors, and other natural phenomena were omens of evil
   (C) "forecast," and alludes to the fact that the behavior of insects can be used to predict the next day's weather
   (D) "imitate," and suggests that glowworms mimic the cyclical flight of comets
   (E) "weigh," and makes clear that glowworms are oblivious to the dramatic upheavals of human life

GO ON TO THE NEXT PAGE

37. Which of the following best expresses the meaning of "higher end" (line 7) ?

    (A) brighter level
    (B) greater distance off the ground
    (C) further boundary
    (D) secret intention
    (E) nobler purpose

38. Which of the following is the closest synonym for "officious," as it is used in line 9 ?

    (A) helpful
    (B) dim
    (C) wandering
    (D) bureaucratic
    (E) meddlesome

39. The speaker implies that, without the glowworms, mowers who have "lost their aim" (line 11) would be likely to

    (A) mow the wrong fields
    (B) conduct themselves disgracefully
    (C) fall in love
    (D) be distracted by other, mysterious sources of light
    (E) never find their way home

40. Which of the following is the best paraphrase for the last line of the poem?

    (A) I am blinded by my resentment toward her.
    (B) I will continue wandering forever.
    (C) I will never be myself again.
    (D) I will never go home without her.
    (E) I will never go to heaven.

41. The main verb in the sentence that states the overall theme of the poem is

    (A) "sit" (line 2)
    (B) "waste" (line 13)
    (C) "come" (line 14)
    (D) "displaced" (line 15)
    (E) "find" (line 16)

42. "The Mower to the Glowworms" could most reasonably be considered

    (A) a celebration of fireflies
    (B) an elaborate compliment to a woman
    (C) an analysis of love at first sight
    (D) an allegory about the Holy Spirit
    (E) a commentary on the foolishness of mowers

GO ON TO THE NEXT PAGE

Questions 43-53. Read the following passage carefully before you choose your answers.

ROSE: Times have changed since you was playing baseball, Troy. That was before the war. Times have changed a lot since then.

TROY: How in hell they done changed?

5 ROSE: They got lots of colored boys playing ball now. Baseball and football.

BONO: You right about that, Rose. Times have changed, Troy. You just come along too early.

10 TROY: There ought not never have been no time called too early! Now you take that fellow . . . what's that fellow they had playing right field for the Yankees back then? You know who I'm talking about, Bono. Used to play right field for the Yankees.

15

ROSE: Selkirk?

TROY: Selkirk! That's it! Man batting .269, understand? .269. What kind of sense that 20 make? I was hitting .432 with thirty-seven home runs! Man batting .269 and playing right field for the Yankees! I saw Josh Gibson's* daughter yesterday. She walking around with raggedy shoes on her feet. 25 Now I bet you Selkirk's daughter ain't walking around with raggedy shoes on her feet! I bet you that!

ROSE: They got a lot of colored baseball players now. Jackie Robinson was the first. Folks 30 had to wait for Jackie Robinson.

TROY: I done seen a hundred niggers play baseball better than Jackie Robinson. Hell, I know some teams Jackie Robinson couldn't even make! Jackie Robinson wasn't nobody. 35 I'm talking about if you could play ball then they ought to have let you play. Don't care what color you were. Come telling me I come along too early. If you could play . . . then they ought to have let you play.

40 *(Troy takes a long drink from the bottle.)*

ROSE: You gonna drink yourself to death. You don't need to be drinking like that.

TROY: Death ain't nothing. I done seen him. Done wrastled with him. You can't tell me nothing 45 about death. Death ain't nothing but a fastball on the outside corner. And you know what I'll do to that! Lookee here, Bono . . .

am I lying? You get one of them fastballs, about waist height, over the outside corner of the plate where you can get the meat of the 50 bat on it . . . and good god! You can kiss it goodbye. Now, am I lying?

BONO: Naw, you telling the truth there. I seen you do it.

TROY: If I'm lying . . . that 450 feet worth of 55 lying! *(Pause.)* That's all death is to me. A fastball on the outside corner.

ROSE: I don't know why you want to get on talking about death.

TROY: Ain't nothing wrong with talking about 60 death. That's part of life. Everybody gonna die. You gonna die, I'm gonna die. Bono's gonna die. Hell, we all gonna die.

(1986)

*Josh Gibson was a notable baseball player in the Negro Leagues.

43. It can be inferred that Troy played baseball

(A) before the outbreak of World War I
(B) long before the period in which Selkirk played right field for the Yankees
(C) before Jackie Robinson was born
(D) before the major leagues were racially integrated
(E) until his near brush with death

44. Which of the following best expresses the meaning of Troy's statement that "There ought not never have been no time called too early!" (lines 10-11) ?

(A) We should judge past conditions in light of their historical context.
(B) It is a shame that we must wait for society's flaws to be corrected by progress and social change.
(C) Most individuals are born before the time period in which they could most prosper or succeed.
(D) The language we use to describe the world affects the way we experience the world.
(E) Despite the appearance of progress, social conditions do not really improve.

GO ON TO THE NEXT PAGE

45. Troy mentions his encounter with Josh Gibson's daughter to

    (A) prove that Selkirk had been unqualified to play right field for the Yankees
    (B) cite an example of a black athlete whose skills in his view exceeded those of Jackie Robinson
    (C) pay tribute to the greatest of right fielders in the Negro Leagues
    (D) illustrate the disparity in the economic rewards available to white and to black professional baseball players before the integration of Major League Baseball
    (E) emphasize his point that times have not changed

46. Troy's tone in lamenting the injustice of his baseball career is one of

    (A) evenhanded objectivity
    (B) harsh political fervor
    (C) lingering resentment
    (D) naïve idealism
    (E) pompous self-pity

47. Troy begins a speech by personifying death and then proceeds to

    (A) ignore Rose's well-meaning advice
    (B) revert to his previous bragging about his prowess as a baseball player
    (C) make a comparison expressing his fearlessness of death
    (D) make an analogy that shows that he believes he can evade death
    (E) explain what he believes it will feel like to die

48. Which of the following stylistic devices are employed by the playwright to evoke the atmosphere of the scene?

    I. soliloquy
    II. double entendre
    III. nonstandard English

    (A) I only
    (B) II only
    (C) III only
    (D) I and III only
    (E) II and III only

49. Troy's attitude toward death is primarily one of

    (A) contemptuous denial
    (B) naïve self-delusion
    (C) boastful nonchalance
    (D) awed anticipation
    (E) thinly veiled cowardice

50. From the passage, it can be inferred that Troy and Bono are

    (A) opponents in a long-standing dispute
    (B) former teammates of Josh Gibson
    (C) baseball players of two different generations
    (D) flirtatious colleagues
    (E) old friends

51. Rose's role in the passage can best be described as

    (A) inquisitive
    (B) condemning
    (C) justifying
    (D) instigating
    (E) attentive

52. It can be inferred that Rose's feelings for Troy are characterized by

    (A) affectionate concern
    (B) sarcastic mockery
    (C) reverent admiration
    (D) apathetic dismissal
    (E) jealous anxiety

53. Which of the following would most logically precede the discussion excerpted in this passage?

    (A) A discussion about whether Troy's son can expect to be discriminated against in his sports career because he is black
    (B) A debate over whether Troy should compete for a spot at the Yankees' spring training camp
    (C) A debate over the merits of racially integrated neighborhoods
    (D) A discussion of the great moments in Troy's baseball career
    (E) A discussion of persistent racial unrest in American society

GO ON TO THE NEXT PAGE

Questions 54-61. Read the following passage carefully before you choose your answers.

    The guest waked from a dream, and
remembering his day's pleasure hurried to dress
himself that it might sooner begin. He was
sure from the way the shy little girl looked
5 once or twice yesterday that she had at least
seen the white heron, and now she must really
be persuaded to tell. Here she comes now,
paler than ever, and her worn old frock is torn
and tattered, and smeared with pine pitch. The
10 grandmother and the sportsman stand in the
door together and question her, and the
splendid moment has come to speak of the dead
hemlock-tree by the green marsh.
    But Sylvia does not speak after all, though
15 the old grandmother fretfully rebukes her, and
the young man's kind appealing eyes are
looking straight in her own. He can make them
rich with money; he has promised it, and they
are poor now. He is so well worth making
20 happy, and he waits to hear the story she can
tell.
    No, she must keep silence! What is it that
suddenly forbids her and makes her dumb? Has
she been nine years growing, and now, when
25 the great world for the first time puts out a
hand to her, must she thrust it aside for a bird's
sake? The murmur of the pine's green branches
in her ears, she remembers how the white heron
came flying through the golden air and how
30 they watched the sea and the morning together,
and Sylvia cannot speak; she cannot tell the
heron's secret and give its life away.

                    (1886)

54. It can be inferred that the guest's anticipated
"day's pleasure" (line 2) centered around

(A) his furthering his acquaintance with Sylvia
(B) his hearing the end of a tale that Sylvia has
    promised to finish for him
(C) his opportunity to make a carving from a
    petrified hemlock tree
(D) his opportunity to photograph a white heron in
    its natural habitat
(E) his opportunity to shoot a white heron

55. Which of the following is NOT an effect of the
switch from past-tense narration to present-tense
narration in the first paragraph?

(A) It conveys the young man's surprise at the
    little girl's appearance.
(B) It emphasizes the young man's suspense in
    waiting for her to speak.
(C) It serves to heighten the reader's anticipation
    of the little girl's revelation.
(D) It signals the narrator's switch from the
    guest's point of view to the little girl's.
(E) It intensifies the reader's sense that this is a
    moment that both the young man and Sylvia
    have been eagerly awaiting.

56. Which of the following is the strongest enticement
for Sylvia to lead the young man to where she has
seen the white heron?

(A) her grandmother's failing health
(B) her respect for the young man's good
    intentions toward the heron
(C) her fear that the young man might take her
    away from her familiar surroundings
(D) his promise of financial reward
(E) his loyalty to all the wild creatures of the
    region

57. Which of the following best articulates Sylvia's
feelings toward the young man?

(A) She hopes to win his esteem at any cost.
(B) She is torn between her desire to please him
    and her contrary impulse not to assist him.
(C) She is indifferent to his aims and toward him
    as a person.
(D) She is repulsed by him personally, although
    she supports his endeavor.
(E) She despises his mercenary motives.

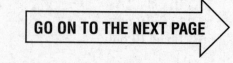

GO ON TO THE NEXT PAGE

58. Sylvia's own surprise at her reluctance to speak is best conveyed by

    (A) the narrator's emphasis on her and her grandmother's poverty
    (B) the narrator's admission that Sylvia had never before had the chance to fulfill someone's hopes as she might have fulfilled the young man's
    (C) the short sentences used to convey the choppiness of Sylvia's thoughts
    (D) Sylvia's memory of the pine tree and the view of the sea
    (E) the author's use of rhetorical questions to express Sylvia's own self-questioning

59. Sylvia is described in the passage as

    (A) surprised at her own morality
    (B) failing to honor a promise she had made to her grandmother
    (C) frustrating any hope she might have had of getting to know the young man better
    (D) persistently dismissive of other people's feelings
    (E) remaining faithful to her long-standing beliefs

60. Which of the following phrases from the passage is most nearly the antithesis of what the white heron represents to Sylvia?

    (A) "torn and tattered" (lines 8-9)
    (B) "splendid moment" (line 12)
    (C) "nine years growing" (line 24)
    (D) "the great world" (line 25)
    (E) "the golden air" (line 29)

61. "The murmur of the pine's green branches" (line 27) is an example of

    (A) personification
    (B) alliteration
    (C) authorial intrusion
    (D) the pathetic fallacy
    (E) poetic license

STOP

**IF YOU FINISH BEFORE TIME IS CALLED, YOU MAY CHECK YOUR WORK ON THIS SECTION ONLY.
DO NOT TURN TO ANY OTHER SECTION IN THE TEST.**

How to Score The Princeton Review
Practice SAT Literature Subject Test

When you take the real exam, the proctors will collect your test booklet and bubble sheet and send your answer sheet to New Jersey where a computer looks at the pattern of filled-in ovals on your answer sheet and gives you a score. We couldn't include even a small computer with this book, so we are providing this more primitive way of scoring your exam.

Determining Your Score

STEP 1   Using the answer key on the next page, determine how many questions you got right and how many you got wrong on the test. Remember, questions that you do not answer do not count as either right or wrong answers.

STEP 2   List the number of right answers here.

(A) _____

STEP 3   List the number of wrong answers here. Now divide that number by 4. (Use a calculator if you're feeling particularly lazy.)

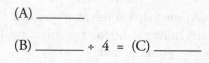

STEP 4   Subtract the number of wrong answers divided by 4 from the number of correct answers. Round this score to the nearest whole number. This is your raw score.

(A) − (C) = _____

STEP 5   To determine your real score, take the number from Step 4 and look it up in the left-hand column of the Score Conversion Table on page 176; the corresponding score on the right is your score on the exam.

Answer Key to Practice SAT Literature Subject Test 2

1.	E	16.	E	31.	B	46.	C
2.	B	17.	B	32.	E	47.	C
3.	D	18.	D	33.	D	48.	C
4.	B	19.	A	34.	C	49.	C
5.	B	20.	D	35.	D	50.	E
6.	B	21.	A	36.	B	51.	C
7.	E	22.	A	37.	E	52.	A
8.	A	23.	B	38.	A	53.	A
9.	C	24.	D	39.	D	54.	E
10.	C	25.	A	40.	C	55.	A
11.	A	26.	C	41.	B	56.	D
12.	E	27.	E	42.	B	57.	B
13.	D	28.	C	43.	D	58.	E
14.	A	29.	D	44.	B	59.	A
15.	C	30.	C	45.	D	60.	D
						61.	A

SAT Literature Subject Test—Score Conversion Table

Raw Score	College Board Scaled Score	Raw Score	College Board Scaled Score
61	800	25	520
60	800	24	510
59	800	23	500
58	800	22	490
57	800	21	490
56	800	20	480
55	790	19	470
54	780	18	460
53	780	17	450
52	770	16	440
51	760	15	430
50	750	14	4120
49	740	13	410
48	730	12	410
47	720	11	400
46	710	10	390
45	700	09	380
44	700	08	370
43	690	07	360
42	680	06	350
41	670	05	350
40	660	04	340
39	650	03	330
38	640	02	320
37	630	01	310
36	620	00	300
35	620	-01	300
34	610	−02	290
33	600	−03	280
32	590	−04	270
31	580	−05	260
30	570	−06	250
29	560	−07	240
28	550	−08	240
27	540	−09	230
26	530	−10	220
		−11	210
		−12	200
		−13	200
		−14	200
		−15	200

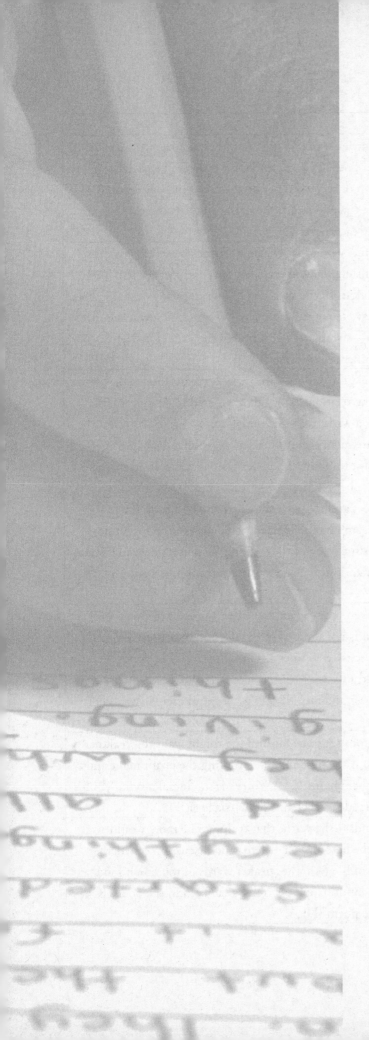

Chapter 16
Practice Test 2:
Answers and Explanations

Answers and Explanations

Question	Answer	Explanation
1	E	The lines "Keep we both our liberties" (line 3) and "Let us be the friends we were" (line 21) suggest that the speaker does not want to be tied down to her listener by marriage (E). There is no mention of secrets (A) or of articles of incorporation (B). No inventory of items is listed in the poem (C); the narrator wants them to be friends, so presumably they'll see each other (D).
2	B	The listener is described as "warm," while the speaker describes herself as "cold," so it is reasonable to infer that the listener feels more than does the speaker (B). The listener is warm so he is not oblivious to the speaker (A), nor does he not reciprocate her feelings (she may not even have feelings for him) (C). There is no evidence that she is incapable of a relationship—she may "once have felt the sun" (D). There is no evidence that she is grieving another relationship (E).
3	D	The last two lines compare the relationship to "fare," which means food (D). The speaker wants to be friends, so the relationship is not compared to strangers (A). Rolling the die is a metaphor for a wedding, which does not occur, so (B) is not the correct answer. No obligations are mentioned (liberties, yes; obligations, no) (C). The speaker says she does not want to know about the past, as symbolized by the crystal ball, but does not compare her relationship to that object (E).
4	B	The speaker talks of past romances and suggests she's had one by saying she has "seen Sunlight," so sunlight is a symbol of love (B). It is not a stand-in for "innocence" (A) or "purity" (C). She is speaking of the past, so the present decision is not the "sunlight" (D). There is no mention that the speaker is thinking about understanding (E).
5	B	By Process of Elimination, a broken promise without the knowledge of the other party is not the correct answer (it is not implied in the poem) (B). Choice (A) is mentioned in lines 7–8; (C) is discussed in lines 17–18. Choice (D) is mentioned in lines 19–20, and (E) is mentioned in lines 13–14. (Note: You should be circling the "NOT" and putting a "Y" for "yes" and an "N" for "no" next to each answer choice to find the odd man out.)
6	B	The speaker worries that if she promises to be faithful she might want to break her vows, so chafing at her bonds (B) is the best answer. Irritating the chain makes no sense (A). She does not "agitate" her chains (C). "Worry" is too literal a synonym for "fret" (D). And she does not "corrode" the chains of marriage (E).
7	E	The speaker wants to just be friends—she warns that trying to be more would destroy the friendship, so (E) is the best answer. There is no discussion of whether people should enjoy the richness of life (A). The speaker warns of too much food, not nothing (B). The diminishment of happiness is not a concern in the poem (C). She does not mention risks in the poem (D).

Question	Answer	Explanation
8	A	The speaker lets the listener down gently, so (A) is the best answer. She does not express disappointment (B), nor is she ambivalent or patronizing (condescending) (C). She is not vague (D), nor is she harsh (E).
9	C	The poem is about broken promises, so (C) is the best answer. The speaker is against promises; they are not "sweet" (A). There is no mention of the filling of promises (B). Answer choice (D) is a too-literal interpretation of the title, and because the speaker's mention of her past, it does not seem as though she denies herself pleasure (E).
10	C	The author is showing how education is best obtained (C). The primary purpose is not to demonstrate the education of the author (A), nor to encourage pupils (he criticizes those who overstudy) (B). He does not rank the motivations for study (D), nor is his main purpose to keep students ethical (E).
11	A	The sentence beginning on line 5 says that some people with only experience, not education, can make decent decisions, but that the overall plans should be made by people who are educated. "Expert" means more "having experience" (A) than literally having learned a trade (B). The "expert men" "judge of particulars," so they are not merely those who carry out the decisions (C). The author speaks of scholars later on in the passage (D). There is no discussion of what kinds of business "expert men" do (E).
12	E	According to the author, just as plants need to be pruned to grow correctly, so too does natural ability need education to flourish properly (E). Plants do not prune themselves, and there is no mention of self-discipline (A). The author does not differentiate between kinds of students (B). He speaks of having to tame natural abilities, not having to foster them (C). The author does not talk about making all individuals the same (D).
13	D	The only answer choice not mentioned in the passage is (D), that scholars should live according to the morals they find in their studies. (A) is mentioned in lines 7–9, while (B) is talked about in lines 9–10. Lines 10–11 caution against showing off (C), and (E) is discussed in lines 16–17. (Note: You should circle the word "NOT" and put a "Y" for "yes" and an "N" for "no" next to each answer choice to find the odd man out.)
14	A	The "simple men" referred to are very impressed with studies (A). There is no evidence that they respect people who are educated (B), nor that they enjoy studies (C). Although answer choice (D) is tempting, there is no evidence that simple men want to have studies, but just that they are impressed by them (D). There is no evidence in the passage that simple men are drawn toward studies (E).

Question	Answer	Explanation
15	C	The author mostly compares lists of qualities in each sentence, balancing the opposing parts, so (C) is the best answer. The only metaphor in the passage is the comparison to plants (A). The author does not use hyperbole (exaggeration) (B). There is little alliteration in the piece (D). The sentences are not all convoluted (take the first sentence, for example) (E).
16	E	Lines 21–24 tell the reader to study in order to "weigh and consider" (E). The author warns against reading to "confute," or find opinions (A). No mention is made of moral or religious beliefs (B). Amusement (C) and conversation (D) are mentioned (lines 2–4), but not as the primary reasons for reading.
17	B	The author is trying to teach the reader something, so the tone can best be described as "didactic" (designed to teach) (B). The narrator is not devout or religious (A), nor is he "satiric" (C). The narrator does not mention ethics or morals in the passage (D), nor does he argue with any other viewpoint (E).
18	D	The father and the boy are testing each other in this poem, changing their relationship as the boy grows, so (D) is the best answer. The errand on which the father sends the son is not a rite of passage, nor do we know the age of the boy (A). It is not a contest of wills because the boy and his father are smiling (B). The focus of the poem is not on the errand, but on the boy's reaction to it (C). The poet remembers the exchange fondly, so there is no evidence of resentment (E).
19	A	The father asks for things that don't have any relationship. Even if this is difficult to see, (A) is the only answer that can't be eliminated. We don't know what the father's work is, and these things cannot be tools (B). Choice (C) is a too-literal interpretation of "fool's errand." The errand is more specifically about the boy and his father, not about degrees of understanding in general (D). The father is not asking for the son to find common ground; the common ground is an outcome of the errand (E).
20	D	The only one of these answers not found in the poem is (D)—there is a metaphor in the second stanza comparing the errand to a game, and calling the task a "fool's errand." Even if you don't know perfect rhyme from slant rhyme, the rhyme scheme changes between the two stanzas (A). The speaker is the father in the first stanza and his son in the second (B). The narrator is obviously remembering an event that happened in the past (C), and the switch is from the words that he remembers to the thoughts he first had upon hearing those words (E). (Note: You should circle the word "NOT" and put a "Y" for "yes" and an "N" for "no" next to each answer choice to find the odd man out.)
21	A	Although the father wanted the boy to go on the errand, his smile at the end shows he was pleased with the boy, so (A) is the best answer. We cannot predict what will happen in the future (B), (C). The father expressed his gladness with a smile (D), so he presumably was not disappointed (E).

Question	Answer	Explanation
22	A	By "putting it up to him," the boy is showing that he realizes the errand is not meant to be completed, so he understands the joke (A). There is no challenge issued to the father (B), nor is the boy particularly defiant (C). He does not go on the errand, so he cannot hand his father the items (D). And he does not turn the joke back around (E).
23	B	"Trumped" refers to a card game wherein one wins the hand by playing a card of the "trump" suit (such as in Bridge, Hearts, or Whist) (B). Don't confuse "trumped" with "trumpeted" (A). There is no showiness or finery mentioned in the poem (C). There is no footstomping in the poem (D). The boy has gained an advantage in the game, but he has not overshadowed his father completely (E).
24	D	"The next move in the game" suggests that the game will continue, so (D) is the best answer. We can't know what the nature of the next form of teasing will be (A). There is no evidence that the father wants to make his son appear ridiculous; rather, he is harmlessly teasing his son (B). There is no evidence that the father will delay his response (C). We cannot predict how long this game will last (E).
25	A	"Negro eyes" refers to the black people watching the funeral (A). White people are not the ones watching (B). The funeral refers to the finest event in general, not the finest-looking people (C). There is no mention of what white funerals are like (D). There is no evidence that there were any white people in attendance at the funeral (E).
26	C	All of the community's important people came to Joe's funeral, so he must have been well regarded (C). Janie does not necessarily feel genuine grief, and she's not mentioned in the first paragraph (A). There is no information in the passage about Joe's life (B). There is no generalization being drawn from this particular funeral (D) and (E).
27	E	Janie's outside appearance gives no clue to her inner feelings: "She sent her face to Joe's funeral, and herself went rollicking with the springtime across the world"; so she is detached (E). We do not know what the mourners are really feeling (A) and (B). We cannot judge their sincerity (C). And we don't know enough to be able to tell if they are a single community (D).
28	C	To be in the secret orders, you must be "initiated," and they are wearing certain colors, so it is reasonable to assume that they are members of a fraternal organization (C). There is only one car mentioned (A). There is nothing in the passage about governing commands (B). There is no evidence that anyone at the funeral was a stranger (D). There is no mention of heaven or life after death (E).
29	D	Janie is obviously not grieving at Joe's death, and her veil allows her to go to the funeral without letting on (D). Janie is not anguished (A). No one is staring at her accusingly (B). Janie's emotional state cannot be described as "solid" (C). Janie knows what her true feelings are (E).

Question	Answer	Explanation
30	C	Everyone is celebrating, but Janie is not; she is isolated (C). The funeral does not emphasize Joe's life (A). The primary effect of the phrase is not to emphasize the "community" of the funeral (B). There is no mention of distances traveled (D). There is no larger lesson that the passage is attempting to draw parallels to (E).
31	B	The most obvious style is the use of incomplete sentences (B). There is no dialect in the passage (A), nor is there much religious imagery (C). There are no ironies in the passage (D), and although there are some contrasts, there are no oxymorons (E).
32	E	Janie is herself behind the veil, which is described as "resurrection and life" (E). "Gloat and glamor" refers to the secret orders (A); "starched and ironed" refers to Janie's outward appearance (B). "Darkness. Deep hole" refers to the funeral proceedings, not Janie's emotions (C); she is not "weeping and wailing" (D).
33	D	Janie feels as though she is reborn, brought to life by Joe's death (lines 25–26) (D). Janie is inwardly celebrating, so his death has had some effect on her (A). We have no evidence that Janie cared for Joe (B). We don't know Janie's exact feelings, but she feels calm, not antipathetic (C). We have no evidence that the community knows or doesn't know about Janie's feelings for Joe (E).
34	C	The poet calls the glowworms "lamps" (line 1), "comets" (line 5), "flame" (line 9), and "lights" (line 13), so they are naturally luminous (shining) (C). There is no mention of glowworms' intelligence (A) or of their tranquility (B). They are not inconsequential (D), and there is no mention of their death (E).
35	D	The glowworms help the nightingale (line 2) (Statement I) and the mowers (line 10) (Statement III), but not the princes (Statement II). Answer choice (D) is correct.
36	B	The word "portend" means to predict, and the author is drawing attention to the glowworms' innocence to show that, unlike comets, they do not foretell evil (the superstition is elucidated by the line "No war nor prince's funeral") (B). The poet says the glowworms do NOT foretell future events (A). There is no weather mentioned (C). There is no mention of a cyclical flight pattern (D). The word "portend" cannot mean "weigh" in this context (E).
37	E	The glowworms' light is not of great importance or nobler purpose than to shed light (E). Answer choice (A) is a too-literal interpretation of the phrase, as is answer choice (B). Answer choice (C) does not make sense in this context, and there is no "secret intention" (D).
38	A	The glowworm is helping to light the mower's way (A). If the mower can see by it, it must not be dim (B). The mower is wandering, not the light (C). There is no evidence that the "officious flame" is bureaucratic (D) or that it is interfering (E).

Question	Answer	Explanation
39	D	The speaker says that mowers "after foolish fires do stray," meaning they follow other sources of light (D). They would not mow other fields (A) or display poor manners (B). There is no evidence that they would fall in love without the glowworms (C), and although the speaker might never find his way home, it is not because there are no glowworms (E).
40	C	His mind is so displaced by thoughts of Juliana that it will never go back to its original state (C). He is not resentful (A). He wanders metaphorically, not literally (B), so home is metaphoric, too (D). There is no mention of heaven (E).
41	B	The question asks for the main verb in the main idea sentence. The first three stanzas are all addressed to the glowworms ("Ye glowworms who . . . who . . . who . . .") and do not state the main idea. Not until the fourth stanza does the reader get to the main-idea sentence ("Your courteous lights . . ."). The main verb in this sentence—the verb that belongs with the subject "glowworms"— is "waste." So, the best answer is (B). "Sit" refers to the nightingales, not the main subject (A); "come" refers to Juliana, not the main subject (C). "Displaced" is a verb attached to Juliana (D), and the verb "find" refers to the narrator, not the glowworms (E).
42	B	The whole poem is stating that although the glowworms are powerful lights, they are nothing compared to Juliana, so (B) is the best answer. The poem is not a celebration of fireflies (A). The poem does not mention love at first sight (C). There is no evidence of religious allegory (D), and the fires are what are considered foolish, not the mowers (which is not the main point of the poem anyway) (E).
43	D	Troy wasn't allowed to play baseball because he was African American, so he must have played before the major leagues were racially integrated (D). There is no mention of when exactly Troy played (before or after World War I) (A), so we can't know how long before Selkirk played (B). Jackie Robinson might already have been born when Troy played baseball, but Robinson hadn't yet broken the color barrier (C). There is no mention of Troy's brush with death (E).
44	B	Troy thinks that there never should have been a rule that prevented him from playing baseball—that he couldn't play because society hadn't progressed enough (B). He does not think that history should be excused just because of its context (A). Choice (C) is not true, as Jackie Robinson prospered as a baseball player. There is no discussion of language (D). The statement quoted does not mention whether social conditions have really improved (E).

Question	Answer	Explanation
45	D	Gibson was a famous baseball player, but his daughter was poor, so there is a large difference between the money that white players and African American players earned before Major League Baseball was integrated (D). The encounter with Gibson's daughter has nothing to do with Selkirk's qualifications (A). The point of the anecdote was to show the disparate salaries, not to compare black athletes (B). There is no tribute being paid (C). He is not saying that times have not changed—now African Americans can play in the major leagues (E).
46	C	Troy is still upset that he did not become a professional baseball player: ".269. What kind of sense that make? I was hitting .432 with thirty-seven home runs" (lines 18–20), so (C) is the best answer. He is neither objective (A), nor particularly politically active (B). He is pessimistic, not idealistic (D). He is not pompous or self-pitying (E), but rather angry.
47	C	Troy compares death to a fastball that he hits out of the park, meaning he does not fear death (C). He does not begin his speech and then ignore Rose's advice (A), and the point of his speech is not to boast (B). He does not believe he can evade death: "I'm gonna die" (line 62) (D). The speech does not say how he thinks death will feel (E).
48	C	The characters use nonstandard English throughout the passage (Statement III). The author does not use soliloquy (where the character speaks aloud as though talking to himself) because the speeches are all directed at other characters (Statement I). There are no double entendres (words or phrases with more than one meaning) (Statement II).
49	C	Troy thinks death is like a fastball—you gotta take what's coming—so (C) is the best answer. He knows he's going to die, so he's not in denial (A), nor is he delusional (B). He is not anxiously awaiting death, nor is he in awe of it (D) or afraid of it (E).
50	E	Troy and Bono are old friends—Bono knew him when Troy was a baseball player (E). They don't seem to be in a dispute (A). There is no evidence they played on a team with Gibson (B). There is not enough information to prove that they are of different generations (C). They are not flirtatious (D).
51	C	Rose keeps trying to explain that baseball is now integrated, so her attitude is justifying (A). She asks only one question; inquisitive does not describe her attitude as a whole (B). She does not stir up trouble (D). She is not particularly attentive; she keeps trying to change the subject.
52	A	In lines 41–42, Rose says, "You don't need to be drinking like that." She is fond of Troy and doesn't want him to hurt himself, so (A) is the best answer. She is not making fun of him (B), nor does she look up to him (C). She is not apathetic (D), and she is not jealous or anxious (E).

Question	Answer	Explanation
53	A	The discussion begins with how times have changed, so it's logical that it would follow a discussion about Troy's son's prospects of becoming a professional athlete (A). Troy is presumably too old (and too drunk) to compete as an athlete (B). They are not discussing the mix of races in neighborhoods (C). If they had been discussing Troy's accomplishments, he would not have reiterated them in the passage (D). They are not discussing current society as a whole, but rather the racial integration of baseball (E).
54	E	If Sylvia tells, she will "give its life away"—so the man must want to hunt the heron, as he is a "sportsman" (line 10) (E). He does not want to know Sylvia; he only wants her to tell him her secret (A). Sylvia knows where the white heron is; she is not telling him a tale (B). He wants to know about the heron, not about wood (C). He wants to harm the heron, not to photograph it undisturbed—he is a "sportsman" (line 10) (E).
55	A	The man is not surprised at Sylvia's appearance; he knows that she is coming (A). The man dresses in a hurry, which means he is anxious, so the present tense serves to heighten the suspense he feels (B). The shift does not affect the anticipation on the reader's part by accelerating the pace from past to present (C). Although the point of view is always omniscient, it goes from a view of the man's thoughts and actions to an interior view of Sylvia's feelings (D). Sylvia has been awaiting this moment as an opportunity to earn money and make the men happy ("the splendid moment has come"), and the switch to the present tense intensifies this suspense. (Note: You should be circling the "NOT" and putting a "Y" for "yes" and an "N" for "no" next to each answer choice to find the odd man out.)
56	D	Because "he can make them rich with money" and because her family is so poor (D), Sylvia considers telling him about the heron. There is no mention of her grandmother's health (A). Sylvia does not think the man has good intentions toward the heron. She knows he is a hunter (B). The man does not threaten to take her away (C). He is a hunter, so he is not loyal to animals (E).
57	B	Sylvia decides to tell him and then changes her mind, so (B) is the best answer. She does not want to win his esteem (A). He has money and "kind, appealing eyes" (line 16), so she is not indifferent to him (C). Because of her observation about his eyes, she is not repulsed (D), and she does not support his endeavor. There is no mention that he will gain money from shooting the heron (E).
58	E	Sylvia questions what it is that makes her unable to speak, so (E) is the best answer. Sylvia's surprise at her reluctance has nothing to do with the narrator's description of her poverty (A). It is not clear that she wants to fulfill his hopes so much as be rewarded with money (B). The sentences are not particularly short, nor are her thoughts choppy (C). The memory is a calming image; it does not show her surprise (D).

Question	Answer	Explanation
59	A	She is surprised that she wants to keep silent to help the heron (A). There is no mention of a promise Sylvia made to her grandmother (B). There is no discussion of whether she wants to know the man better or whether her actions prevent her from doing so (C). She is not dismissive in the passage (D). She is surprised at herself, so her beliefs are not long-standing (E).
60	D	The heron and Sylvia experience an intimate morning together, both naïve, experiencing the world for the first time, so "the great world" is most nearly the opposite (D). The heron does not represent new and clean clothing (A), nor is the heron the opposite of a "splendid moment" (B). She does not think the heron is old, so youth is not the opposite (C). The heron does not represent the earth, so the air is not its antithesis (E).
61	A	Pines do not talk, so the phrase is an example of personification. No words begin with the same sounds, so there is no alliteration (B). The author does not intrude into the passage (C). There is no pathetic fallacy (D), and the example is not odd enough to say that the author has broken any "rules of fiction" (E).

Chapter 17
Practice Test 3

PRACTICE SAT LITERATURE
SUBJECT TEST 3

TEST 3

Your responses to the SAT Literature Subject Test questions should be filled in on Test 3 of your answer sheet.

LITERATURE TEST 3

Directions: This test consists of selections from literary works and questions on their content, form, and style. After each passage or poem, choose the best answer to each question and fill in the corresponding oval on the answer sheet.

Note: Pay particular attention to questions that contain the words NOT, LEAST, or EXCEPT.

Questions 1-9. Read the following poem carefully before you choose your answers.

"The Author to Her Book"

Thou ill-formed offspring of my feeble brain,
Who after birth didst by my side remain,
Till snatched from thence by friends, less wise than true,
Who thee abroad, exposed to public view,
5 Made thee in rags, halting to th' press to trudge,
Where errors were not lessened (all may judge).
At thy return my blushing was not small,
My rambling brat (in print) should mother call,
I cast thee by as one unfit for light,
10 Thy visage was so irksome in my sight;
Yet being mine own, at length affection would
Thy blemishes amend, if so I could:
I washed thy face, but more defects I saw,
And rubbing off a spot still made a flaw.
15 I stretched thy joints to make thee even feet,
Yet still thou run'st more hobbling than is meet;
In better dress to trim thee was my mind,
But nought save homespun cloth i' th' house I find.
In this array 'mongst vulgars may'st thou roam.
20 In critic's hands beware thou dost not come,
And take thy way where yet thou art not known;
If for thy father asked, say thou hadst none;
And for thy mother, she alas is poor,
Which caused her thus to send thee out of door.

(1678)

GO ON TO THE NEXT PAGE

1. The word "house" (line 18) is a metaphor for the author's

   (A) attic
   (B) book
   (C) brain
   (D) shame
   (E) store

2. According to the poem, how did the author's manuscript come to be published?

   (A) The press demanded it.
   (B) Her friends took it from her on the sly.
   (C) It was stolen by a publisher.
   (D) She showed it to someone who recommended it for publication.
   (E) The poem does not state its publication history.

3. According to the poem, how does the author feel about her manuscript?

   (A) She is thrilled to see it in print.
   (B) She thinks it is too dark.
   (C) She is annoyed at its childishness.
   (D) She is horrified by it.
   (E) She is embarrassed by its quality.

4. The lines "I stretched thy joints to make thee even feet, Yet still thou run'st more hobbling than is meet," (lines 15-16) refer to the author's attempt to

   (A) make the book rhyme better
   (B) trim the book's extraneous parts
   (C) fix the book's meter
   (D) make sure the book has an even number of pages
   (E) make the book less offensive

5. The poem as a whole can be considered as

   (A) an extended analogy
   (B) a metaphor for parental worries
   (C) a comparison between two media
   (D) a didactic diatribe
   (E) a discursive exercise

6. The author's tone can best be described as

   (A) cheerless
   (B) antipathetic
   (C) dispassionate
   (D) cavalier
   (E) self-deprecating

7. The word "trim" (line 17) most nearly means

   (A) clothe
   (B) cut
   (C) weave
   (D) hobble
   (E) edit

8. According to the poem, a friend "less wise than true" is most likely to

   (A) mean well but act foolishly
   (B) tell lies in his friend's best interest
   (C) cunningly meddle in his friend's affairs
   (D) sacrifice loyalty for opportunity
   (E) falsely accuse his friend because of lack of knowledge

9. Which of the following is NOT a hope expressed by the author?

   (A) The book will not fall into the hands of critics.
   (B) Someone else will claim authorship.
   (C) The book will fall into obscurity.
   (D) She can fix the book's problems through editing.
   (E) She might make some profit.

GO ON TO THE NEXT PAGE

Questions 10-17. Read the following passage carefully before you choose your answers.

The principal object of this Work is to remove the erroneous and discreditable notions current in England concerning this City, in common with every thing else connected with the Colony.
5 We shall endeavour to represent Sydney as it really is—to exhibit its spacious Gas-lit Streets, crowded by an active and thriving Population—its Public Edifices, and its sumptuous Shops, which boldly claim a comparison with those of London
10 itself: and to shew that the Colonists have not been inattentive to matters of higher import, we shall display to our Readers the beautiful and commodious Buildings raised by piety and industry for the use of Religion. It is true, all are not yet
15 in a state of completion; but, be it remembered, that what was done gradually in England, in the course of many centuries, has been here effected in the comparatively short period of sixty years. Our object, in setting forth this Work, is one of no
20 mean moment; and we trust that every Australian, whether this be his native or adopted country, will heartily bid us "God speed!"
It became necessary, after the rebellion of those Colonies now known as the United States, for
25 Britain to send her convicts elsewhere; and the wide, distant, and almost totally unknown regions of Australia, were adjudged most suitable for the purpose. Accordingly, eleven ships, since known in Colonial History as the "First Fleet," sailed for
30 New Holland on the 15th of May, 1787, under the command of Captain Arthur Phillip, and arrived in Botany Bay on the 20th day of January in the following year. Finding the spot in many respects unfit for an infant settlement, and but scantily
35 supplied with water, Captain Phillip determined to explore the coast; and proceeded northward, with a few officers and marines, in three open boats. After passing along a rocky and barren line of shore for several miles, they entered Port Jackson,
40 which they supposed to be of no great dimensions, it having been marked in the chart of Captain Cook as a boat harbour. Their astonishment may be easily imagined when they found its waters gradually expand, and the full proportions of that
45 magnificent harbour (capable of containing the whole navy of Britain) burst upon their view. The site of the intended settlement was no longer a matter of doubt; and, after first landing at Manly Beach… they eventually selected a spot on the
50 banks of a small stream of fresh water, falling into a Cove on the southern side of the estuary….
Sydney, the capital…is situated on the southern shore of Port Jackson, at the distance of seven miles from the Pacific Ocean…. It is built at the
55 head of the far-famed "Cove"; and, with Darling Harbour as its general boundary to the west, extends, in an unbroken succession of houses, for more than two miles in a southerly direction. As a maritime city its site is unrivalled, possessing at
60 least three miles of water frontage, at any part of which vessels of the heaviest burden can safely approach the wharves. The stratum on which it stands is chiefly sandstone; and, as it enjoys a considerable elevation, it is remarkably healthy
65 and dry. The principal thoroughfares run north and south, parallel to Darling Harbour, and are crossed at right angles by shorter streets. This, at first, gives the place an air of unpleasing sameness and formality, to those accustomed to the winding and
70 romantic streets of an ancient English town; but the eye soon becomes reconciled to the change, and you cease to regret the absence of what is in so many respects undesirable.

(1848)

10. The "Colonists" (line 10) are most likely

(A) prisoners
(B) readers
(C) British sailors
(D) Sydney's citizens
(E) American observers

11. The sentence "It is true, all are not yet in a state of completion; but, be it remembered, that what was done gradually in England, in the course of many centuries, has been here effected in the comparatively short period of sixty years" (lines 14-18) serves which of the following purposes in the passage?

(A) It admits a flaw and accepts the argument.
(B) It outlines a counterargument and then provides justification.
(C) It argues a new point and then returns to the main theme.
(D) It explains a previous point, giving the history behind the argument.
(E) It compares two cities and finds one superior.

GO ON TO THE NEXT PAGE

12. The phrase "mean moment" (line 20) can best be rephrased as

    (A) evil intent
    (B) unhappy time
    (C) average length
    (D) routine description
    (E) small importance

13. The main differences between the three paragraphs can be best described as

    (A) paragraph one addresses the reader, paragraph two continues the argument, and paragraph three summarizes the passage so far
    (B) paragraph one sets the passage's goals, paragraph two tells a history, and paragraph three describes an actual situation
    (C) paragraph one begins the history, paragraph two continues it, and paragraph three concludes it
    (D) paragraph one is descriptive, paragraph two is historical, and paragraph three relates a narrative
    (E) paragraph one is ornate, paragraph two is more subdued, and paragraph three cites examples

14. The second paragraph implies that

    (A) Australia was unsuitable for habitation
    (B) Captain Phillip did not have the backing of the British government
    (C) before the American revolution, Britain used to send its prisoners to America
    (D) Australia had never before been visited by the British
    (E) the "First Fleet" encountered an existing city near Manly Beach.

15. Which of the following is NOT a characteristic of Sydney, according to the passage?

    (A) religious buildings
    (B) perpendicular side streets
    (C) a long coastline
    (D) a shallow harbor
    (E) good weather

16. The final sentence, "This, at first, gives the place an air of unpleasing sameness and formality, to those accustomed to the winding and romantic streets of an ancient English town; but the eye soon becomes reconciled to the change, and you cease to regret the absence of what is in so many respects undesirable," most nearly means

    (A) at first, Sydney seems homogenous to people who like England's historical curved streets, but once you get used to it you stop thinking that windy streets are a good thing
    (B) at first, Sydney seems overly formal to people who have studied England's history, but eventually you grow accustomed to it and stop noticing it
    (C) at first, Sydney seems unpleasant to English visitors, but once they accept Sydney for what it is, they grow to love it
    (D) at first, Sydney's streets seem too similar to England's streets; but once you get to know Sydney you find that's not the case
    (E) at first, Sydney seems too rigid to fans of England's historical curved streets, and people are at first apt to regret their visit to Sydney

17. It is reasonable to infer that the author of the passage

    (A) worries that he or she does not have the full support of Australia's citizens
    (B) believes that Sydney is better than London
    (C) supports urban planning
    (D) is sensitive about his native land
    (E) finds Sydney quaint

GO ON TO THE NEXT PAGE

Questions 18-27. Read the following passage carefully before you choose your answers.

Enter a Roman and a Volsce [meeting].

ROMAN: I know you well, sir, and you know me. Your name, I think, is Adrian.

VOLSCE: It is so, sir. Truly, I have forgot you.

ROMAN: I am a Roman; and my services are, as you are, against 'em. Know you me yet?

5

VOLSCE: Nicanor, no?

ROMAN: The same, sir.

VOLSCE: You had more beard when I last saw you; but your favor is well appear'd by your tongue. What's the news in Rome? I have a note from the Volscian state to find you out there. You have well sav'd me a day's journey.

10

ROMAN: There hath been in Rome strange insurrections; the people against the senators, patricians, and nobles.

15

VOLSCE: Hath been? Is it ended, then? Our state thinks not so. They are in a most warlike preparation, and hope to come upon them in the heat of their division.

20

ROMAN: The main blaze of it is past, but a small thing would make it flame again; for the nobles receive so to heart the banishment of that worthy Coriolanus that they are in a ripe aptness to take all power from the people and to pluck from them their tribunes forever. This lies glowing, I can tell you, and is almost mature for the violent breaking out.

25

VOLSCE: Coriolanus banish'd?

30

ROMAN: Banish'd, sir.

VOLSCE: You will be welcome with this intelligence, Nicanor.

ROMAN: The day serves well for them now. I have heard it said, the fittest time to corrupt a man's wife is when she's fall'n out with her husband. Your noble Tullus Aufidius will appear well in these wars, his great opposer, Coriolanus, being now in no request of his country.

35

40

VOLSCE: He cannot choose. I am most fortunate, thus accidentally to encounter you. You have ended my business, and I will merrily accompany you home.

45

ROMAN: I shall, between this and supper, tell you most strange things from Rome, all tending to the good of their adversaries. Have you an army ready, say you?

VOLSCE: A most royal one: the centurions and their charges, distinctly billeted, already in th' entertainment, and to be on foot at an hour's warning.

50

ROMAN: I am joyful to hear of their readiness, and am the man, I think, that shall set them in present action. So, sir, heartily well met, and most glad of your company.

55

VOLSCE: You take my part from me, sir; I have the most cause to be glad of yours.

ROMAN: Well, let us go together.

[Exeunt.] (1623)

18. The meeting between the two men can best be described as

(A) cordial and heartwarming
(B) melodramatic and saccharine
(C) acrimonious and awkward
(D) scandalous and surprising
(E) fortuitous and serendipitous

19. The character of Nicanor is

(A) a Roman spying for the Volscians
(B) Adrian's distant cousin
(C) Adrian's rival for the attentions of a woman
(D) a mercenary in search of Coriolanus
(E) a sworn enemy of Adrian

20. The insurrections spoken of in line 15 are most likely

(A) foreign invasions
(B) military coups
(C) monarchical successions
(D) proletariat uprisings
(E) conflagrations

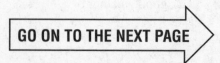
GO ON TO THE NEXT PAGE

21. It can be inferred from the passage that

    (A) Coriolanus's banishment is the cause of the insurrection
    (B) Coriolanus's banishment was not the nobles' choice
    (C) Coriolanus was the king of Rome
    (D) the two men are supporters of Coriolanus
    (E) the two men dread further war

22. "The main blaze" (line 21) refers to

    (A) a universally quelled rebellion
    (B) public outrage at Coriolanus's banishment
    (C) the fires of purgatory
    (D) incendiary comments
    (E) the people's revolt

23. The plot the men hatch hinges on the fact that

    (A) Tullus Aufidius is romantically involved with Coriolanus's wife
    (B) Roman towns catch fire easily
    (C) the nobles are incensed that Coriolanus has been banished
    (D) there is a ready army
    (E) the senators and patricians are not ready for war

24. The line "You take my part from me, sir" could best be restated as

    (A) "Those were the words I was going to speak"
    (B) "You have usurped my role"
    (C) "You are making fun of me"
    (D) "I would give you a present for your kindness"
    (E) "Yours is the friendship I most cherish"

25. It can be inferred from the passage that the author intended this play most likely to be

    (A) an amusing comedy
    (B) an extended allegory
    (C) a pastoral study
    (D) a historical enactment
    (E) a political satire

26. The words "appear well" (line 38) can best be replaced by

    (A) fight valiantly
    (B) dress for battle
    (C) emerge victorious
    (D) argue persuasively
    (E) feign health

27. This passage is included in the play most likely

    (A) to serve as a backdrop for a romantic interlude
    (B) to provide comic relief
    (C) to impart information
    (D) to pander to the audience's interests
    (E) to show the audience the ambience of ancient Rome

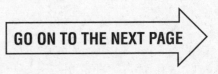

Questions 28-36. Read the following poem carefully before you choose your answers.

"We Too Shall Sleep"

Not, not for thee,
Belovèd child, the burning grasp of life
Shall bruise the tender soul. The noise, and
   strife,
5 And clamor of midday thou shalt not see;
But wrapped for ever in thy quiet grave,
Too little to have known the earthly lot,
Time's clashing hosts above thine innocent head,
Wave upon wave,
10 Shall break, or pass as with an army's tread,
And harm thee not.

A few short years
We of the living flesh and restless brain
Shall plumb the deeps of life and know the
15   strain,
The fleeting gleams of joy, the fruitless tears;
And then at last when all is touched and tried,
Our own immutable night shall fall, and deep
In the same silent plot, O little friend,
20 Side by thy side,
In peace that changeth not, nor knoweth end,
We too shall sleep.

                        (1899)

28. All of the following are examples of personification EXCEPT

    (A) "burning grasp" (line 2)
    (B) "bruise" (line 3)
    (C) "clashing" (line 8)
    (D) "break" (line 10)
    (E) "tread" (line 10)

29. A difference between the first and second stanzas is

    (A) stanza one speaks of memory, while stanza two speaks of the future
    (B) stanza one speaks of death, while stanza two speaks of slumber
    (C) stanza one speaks of day, while stanza two speaks of night
    (D) stanza one speaks of children, while stanza two speaks of the past
    (E) stanza one speaks of hurry, while stanza two speaks of patience

30. Which of the following lines contains a simile?

    (A) "But wrapped for ever in thy quiet grave,/ Too little to have known the earthly lot" (lines 6-7)
    (B) "Shall break, or pass as with an army's tread,/ And harm thee not" (lines 10-11)
    (C) "We of the living flesh and restless brain/ Shall plumb the deeps of life and know the strain" (lines 13-15)
    (D) "And then at last when all is touched and tried,/ Our own immutable night shall fall, and deep" (lines 17-18)
    (E) The poem does not contain a simile.

31. The title symbolically represents

    (A) slumber
    (B) burial
    (C) angels
    (D) death
    (E) old age

GO ON TO THE NEXT PAGE

32. The author's attitude toward life can best be described as

    (A) life must be endured before death sets us free
    (B) life is sometimes good and sometimes difficult, but it is always short
    (C) life is merely noisy and full of strife
    (D) life is too difficult to be enjoyed
    (E) life's meaning will be forever obscured

33. From the passage, it can be inferred that the author considers that

    (A) it is better to be dead than to suffer fate's cruelty
    (B) death is akin to unconsciousness
    (C) death is like being swept away by waves
    (D) death is the same for soldiers as for children
    (E) it is ridiculous to cry tears for the dead

34. The poem is written from the point of view of

    (A) someone who is grieving
    (B) a congregation of mourners
    (C) someone who is dying
    (D) someone who fears death
    (E) someone who has never before been touched by death

35. Which of the following ideas is NOT implied by the poem?

    (A) Life is joyfully or harshly noisy.
    (B) Death is quiet and peaceful.
    (C) Time is like the ocean.
    (D) Life is alternately wonderful and painful.
    (E) The afterlife is superior to our earthly existence.

36. The words "touched and tried" (line 17) represent

    (A) experience
    (B) intensity
    (C) justice
    (D) eternal life
    (E) fruitlessness

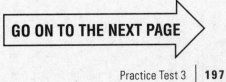

GO ON TO THE NEXT PAGE

Questions 37-46. Read the following passage carefully before you choose your answers.

There comes to the house of Yen Chow a Chinese merchant of wealth and influence. His eyes dwell often upon Ah Leen. He whispers to her father. Yen Chow puffs his pipe and muses:
5 Assuredly a great slight has been put upon his family. A divorce would show proper pride. It was not the Chinese way, but was not the old order passing away and the new order taking its place? Aye, even in China, the old country that had
10 seemed as if it would ever remain old. He speaks to Ah Leen.
"Nay, father, nay," she returns. "Thou hadst the power to send my love away from me, but thou canst not compel me to hold out my arms to
15 another."
"But," protests her mother, "thy lover hath forgotten thee. Another hath borne him a child."
A flame rushes over Ah Leen's face; then she becomes white as a water lily. She plucks a leaf of
20 scented geranium, crushes it between her fingers and casts it away. The perfume clings to the hands she lays on her mother's bosom.
"Thus," says she, "the fragrance of my crushed love will ever cling to Ming Hoan."
25 It is evening. The electric lights are shining through the vines. Out of the gloom beyond their radius comes a man. The American girl, seated in a quiet corner of the veranda, sees his face. It is eager and the eyes are full of love and fate. Then
30 she sees Ah Leen. Tired of women's gossip, the girl has come to gaze upon the moon, hanging in the sky above her like a pale yellow pearl.
There is a cry from the approaching man. It is echoed by the girl. In a moment she is leaning
35 upon his breast.
"Ah!" she cries, raising her head and looking into his eyes. "I knew that though another had bound you by human ties, to me you were linked by my love divine."
40 "Another! Human ties!" exclaims the young man. He exclaims without explaining—for the sins of parents must not be uncovered—why there has been silence between them for so long. Then he lifts her face to his and gently reproaches her. "Ah
45 Leen, you have dwelt only upon your love for me. Did I not bid thee, 'Forget not to remember that *I* love thee!'"
The American girl steals away. The happy Ming Hoan is unaware that as she flits lightly by him and
50 his bride she is repeating to herself his words, and hoping that it is not too late to send to someone a message of recall.

(1910)

37. The story takes place most likely in

   (A) China in the twentieth century
   (B) America in the eighteenth century
   (C) China in the eighteenth century
   (D) America in the twentieth century
   (E) It is impossible to tell from the passage.

38. The line "It was not the Chinese way, but was not the old order passing away and the new order taking its place?" is an example of

   (A) indirect dialogue
   (B) authorial intrusion
   (C) overt symbolism
   (D) character shift
   (E) literary allusion

39. It can be inferred from the passage that

   (A) Ah Leen has disobeyed her father
   (B) Yen Chow is interested only in money
   (C) Ah Leen's lover has not been in contact
       contact with her
   (D) Ah Leen's American friend has stolen her
       lover
   (E) Ah Leen is jealous of her American friend

40. The "great slight" (line 5) of which Yen Chow speaks is

   (A) a divorce
   (B) an abandonment
   (C) an interracial marriage
   (D) a deviation from the old ways
   (E) the disrespect of elders

41. The "perfume" (line 21) serves as a symbol of

   (A) the fragility of human ties
   (B) the passing of time
   (C) the strength of the marriage bond
   (D) the sweetness of mutual love
   (E) the endurance of love

GO ON TO THE NEXT PAGE

42. From the beginning to the end of the passage there is a change in

    (A) point of view
    (B) syntax
    (C) temporal logic
    (D) diction
    (E) theme

43. Paragraph 6 "It is evening . . ." contains an example of

    (A) simile
    (B) personification
    (C) alliteration
    (D) parallelism
    (E) anthropomorphism

44. The last paragraph suggests that

    (A) the American girl is going to tell Ming Hoan's parents of the lovers' reunion
    (B) the American girl has a history with Ming Hoan
    (C) Ming Hoan's words are offensive to the American girl
    (D) Ming Hoan's words have caused the American girl to think about her own relationship in a different light
    (E) Chinese morality is incomprehensible to the American girl

45. Why does Ming Hoan not explain his silence?

    (A) He is afraid of hurting Ah Leen.
    (B) He is embarrassed of the reason.
    (C) He wants to protect their parents.
    (D) He doesn't feel he owes her an explanation.
    (E) Ah Leen does not ask him to explain.

46. The main theme of the story is

    (A) old customs are better than new ones
    (B) two people's love is stronger than circumstance
    (C) true love cannot be extinguished
    (D) absence makes the heart grow fonder
    (E) one can never truly know the heart of another

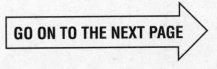

GO ON TO THE NEXT PAGE

Questions 47-54. Read the following poem carefully before you choose your answers.

"The Triumph of Time"

It will grow not again, this fruit of my heart,
Smitten with sunbeams, ruined with rain.
The singing seasons divide and depart,
Winter and summer depart in twain.
5 It will grow not again, it is ruined at root,
The bloodlike blossom, the dull red fruit;
Though the heart yet sickens, the lips yet smart,
With sullen savour of poisonous pain.

I shall never be friends again with roses;
10 I shall loathe sweet tunes, where a note grown strong
Relents and recoils, and climbs and closes,
As a wave of the sea turned back by song.
There are sounds where the soul's delight takes fire,
Face to face with its own desire;
15 A delight that rebels, a desire that reposes;
I shall hate sweet music my whole life long.

The pulse of war and passion of wonder,
The heavens that murmur, the sounds that shine,
The stars that sing and the loves that thunder,
20 The music burning at heart like wine,
An armed archangel whose hands raise up
All senses mixed in the spirit's cup
Till flesh and spirit are molten in sunder—
These things are over, and no more mine.

(1866)

47. The words "Smitten with" (line 2) could best be replaced with

(A) Caressed by
(B) Filtered through
(C) In love with
(D) Awed by
(E) Struck by

48. The poet's attitude in this poem is

(A) resigned
(B) stung
(C) sullen
(D) inured
(E) imperious

49. Which of the following does NOT appear in the poem?
(A) elusive water
(B) an assortment of flora
(C) potent liquor
(D) evocative melody
(E) exotic reverie

50. Which of the following does the first stanza employ?

(A) religious iconography
(B) paired alliteration
(C) melancholic preaching
(D) antipathetic musing
(E) character revelation

51. It is reasonable to assume that the author equates music with

(A) a mocking death
(B) sweet fruit
(C) his lost love
(D) original sin
(E) serpentine slyness

52. All of the following lines contain examples of personification EXCEPT

(A) line 3
(B) line 7
(C) line 20
(D) line 21
(E) line 22

53. The third stanza lists examples of
(A) anecdotal evidence
(B) unpleasant memories
(C) inclement weather
(D) fickle fate
(E) love's intensity

54. Which of the following could replace the last line of the passage?

(A) In love, it's said, one cannot blunder.
(B) Love like an army my heart did plunder.
(C) Neither day nor night can thus resign.
(D) I mourn their passing and decline.
(E) May head and heart now intertwine.

GO ON TO THE NEXT PAGE

Questions 55-61. Read the following passage carefully before you choose your answers.

Once Nanapush began talking, nothing stopped the spill of his words. The day receded and darkness broadened. At dusk, the wind picked up and cold poked mercilessly through the chinking
5 of the cabin. The two wrapped themselves in quilts and continued to talk. The talk broadened, deepened. Went back and forth in time and then stopped time. The talk grew huge, of death and radiance, then shrunk and narrowed to the making
10 of soup. The talk was of madness, the stars, sin, and death. The two spoke of all there was to know. And although it was in English, during the talk itself Nanapush taught language to Father Damien, who took out a small bound notebook and recorded
15 words and sentences.
    In common, they now had the love of music, though their definition of what composed music was dissimilar.
    "When you hear Chopin," Father Damien
20 asserted, "you find yourself traveling into your childhood, then past that, into a time before you were born, when you were nothing, when the only truths you knew were sounds."
    "Ayiih! Tell me, does this Chopin know love
25 songs? I have a few I don't sing unless I mean for sure to capture my woman."
    "This Chopin makes songs so beautiful your knees shake. Dogs cry. The trees moan. Your thoughts fly up nowhere. You can't think. You
30 become flooded in the heart."
    "Powerful. Powerful. This Chopin," asked Nanapush, "does he have a drum?"
    "No," said Damien, "he uses a piano."
    "That great box in your church," said Nanapush.
35 "How is this thing made?"
    Father Damien opened his mouth to say it was constructed of wood, precious woods, but in his mind there formed the image of Agnes's Caramacchione settled in the bed of the river,
40 unmoved by the rush of water over its keys, and instead he said, "Time." As soon as he said it, he knew that it was true.

                                        (2001)

55. The two men are most likely

    (A) old friends
    (B) of different cultures
    (C) future enemies
    (D) negotiators
    (E) members of the clergy

56. The passage moves from
    (A) past to future
    (B) general to specific
    (C) narration to dialogue
    (D) recitation to soliloquy
    (E) complexity to simplicity

57. The word "Ayiih!" (line 24) is an example of
    (A) Father Damien singing
    (B) Father Damien's language
    (C) Chopin's music
    (D) Father Damien's first name
    (E) an interjection

58. The main theme of the passage explores
    (A) cultural differences
    (B) ironic subtext
    (C) the connection between love and music
    (D) the nature of relationships
    (E) the influence of music

59. From the passage, Nanapush's attitude can be described as one of
    (A) intense curiosity
    (B) didactic patronization
    (C) guarded politeness
    (D) affirming sycophancy
    (E) scholarly enthusiasm

60. The phrase "flooded in the heart" (line 30) can best be replaced with
    (A) overcome by joy
    (B) racked with nostalgia
    (C) filled with emotion
    (D) engorged with blood
    (E) momentarily confused

61. In the last paragraph, Father Damien says the piano is made of time because
    (A) he does not know the word for "wood" in Nanapush's language
    (B) wood seemed too banal for so important an instrument
    (C) time seems to be as eternal as the capacity for music
    (D) he once saw a piano in a river
    (E) he is trying to change the subject to one he feels more comfortable with

STOP

**IF YOU FINISH BEFORE TIME IS CALLED, YOU MAY CHECK YOUR WORK ON THIS SECTION ONLY.
DO NOT TURN TO ANY OTHER SECTION IN THE TEST.**

How to Score The Princeton Review
Practice SAT Literature Subject Test

When you take the real exam, the proctors will collect your test booklet and bubble sheet and send your answer sheet to New Jersey where a computer looks at the pattern of filled-in ovals on your answer sheet and gives you a score. We couldn't include even a small computer with this book, so we are providing this more primitive way of scoring your exam.

Determining Your Score

STEP 1   Using the answer key on the next page, determine how many questions you got right and how many you got wrong on the test. Remember, questions that you do not answer do not count as either right or wrong answers.

STEP 2   List the number of right answers here.

(A) _____

STEP 3   List the number of wrong answers here. Now divide that number by 4. (Use a calculator if you're feeling particularly lazy.)

(B) _____ ÷ 4 = (C) _____

STEP 4   Subtract the number of wrong answers divided by 4 from the number of correct answers. Round this score to the nearest whole number. This is your raw score.

(A) – (C) = _____

STEP 5   To determine your real score, take the number from Step 4 and look it up in the left-hand column of the Score Conversion Table on page 204; the corresponding score on the right is your score on the exam.

Answer Key to Practice Sat Literature Subject Test 3

1. C	16. A	31. D	46. B
2. B	17. C	32. B	47. E
3. E	18. E	33. B	48. B
4. C	19. A	34. A	49. E
5. A	20. D	35. E	50. B
6. E	21. B	36. A	51. C
7. A	22. E	37. D	52. B
8. A	23. C	38. A	53. E
9. B	24. A	39. C	54. D
10. D	25. D	40. B	55. B
11. B	26. C	41. E	56. C
12. E	27. C	42. A	57. E
13. B	28. D	43. A	58. E
14. C	29. C	44. D	59. A
15. D	30. B	45. C	60. C
			61. C

SAT Literature Subject Test—Score Conversion Table

Raw Score	College Board Scaled Score	Raw Score	College Board Scaled Score
61	800	25	520
60	800	24	510
59	800	23	500
58	800	22	490
57	800	21	490
56	800	20	480
55	790	19	470
54	780	18	460
53	780	17	450
52	770	16	440
51	760	15	430
50	750	14	4120
49	740	13	410
48	730	12	410
47	720	11	400
46	710	10	390
45	700	09	380
44	700	08	370
43	690	07	360
42	680	06	350
41	670	05	350
40	660	04	340
39	650	03	330
38	640	02	320
37	630	01	310
36	620	00	300
35	620	-01	300
34	610	-02	290
33	600	-03	280
32	590	-04	270
31	580	-05	260
30	570	-06	250
29	560	-07	240
28	550	-08	240
27	540	-09	230
26	530	-10	220
		-11	210
		-12	200
		-13	200
		-14	200
		-15	200

Chapter 18
Practice Test 3:
Answers and Explanations

Answers and Explanations

Question	Answer	Explanation
1	C	Answer choice (C) is correct because the author is racking her brain for ways to make the poem better: "In better dress to trim thee" (line 17). Answers choices (A) and (E) interpret the poem too literally. Choice (B) is incorrect because the author is looking for a way to make the book better. She is not looking for the book itself. Searching in her "shame" does not make sense (D).
2	B	The poem states that the book "didst by my side remain,/Till snatched from thence by friends . . . Who thee abroad, exposed to public view" (lines 2–4) so (B) is the correct answer. The press did not demand the book (A), nor did the publisher steal it (C). There is no evidence that she showed it to anyone (D). And the poem does state how the book came to be published (E).
3	E	The author blushes (line 7), so she is embarrassed, and thus (E) is the correct answer. Embarrassed is not "thrilled" (A). There is no evidence that she feels it is too dark (B), nor that she considers childishness to be one of its faults (C). "Horrified" is too strong a word for how the author feels (D).
4	C	The correct answer is (C). Picture someone hobbling, i.e., walking unevenly. Fixing rhyme will not help the book flow more smoothly (A), but fixing the meter will (C). There is "stretching," so no trimming is involved (B). The "even feet" do not refer to the number of pages (D), and although the book is "irksome" and "vulgar" it is not an offensive book, merely an embarrassing one to the author (E).
5	A	The poem compares a book to a child, so it is an analogy (A). Parental worries are the metaphor, not the poem's point. (B). There is only one medium—the book in question (C). The poem is not intended to instruct, and the word "diatribe" is too strong (D). The poem is not an exercise (E).
6	E	The author makes light of her abilities and relates her struggles to make things better, so her tone is self-deprecating (E). The poem is funny, so she is not cheerless (A). She is not "antipathetic" or "dispassionate" in the poem (B), (C), and a cavalier attitude is one of carelessness, which does not apply (D).
7	A	The word "trim" can be replaced with "dress" as in "to dress someone" (A). Be careful not to use the most obvious definition of trim (B). There is no evidence of weaving (C) or of hobbling (why would she want to hobble her book?) (D). Although the line might be a metaphor for editing, the word itself does not mean edit (E).
8	A	The author says her friends took her book and got it published, so they mean well, but did something foolish (A). There are no lies told in the poem (B). Her friends might meddle, but they are not "cunning" (C). According to the poem, the friends do not gain from the publication (D). There is no evidence that (E) is true.
9	B	The author never hopes that someone else will claim the book (B). She does hope the book will avoid critics (line 18) (A), and that it will be forgotten (line 19) (C). She tries to edit the book, so she hopes it can be fixed (D). She is poor; she hopes she might make some money (lines 23–24) (E).

Question	Answer	Explanation
10	D	The colonists are the people who live in the city of Sydney, "the colony" (D). They are no longer prisoners (A). The colonists are not the readers (B). The colonists are no longer British sailors (C), nor are they American observers (E).
11	B	The paragraph states that Sydney is as important as London. The sentence quoted admits the buildings aren't done, but says that England has had several hundred years to build itself up, while Sydney is only sixty years old—(B) is the best answer. The sentence may admit a flaw, but it does not accept it (A). A new point is not argued (C). The sentence does not explain the previous point (D). The sentence compares England to Australia, but does not say one is superior to the other (E).
12	E	The paragraph is comparing London to Sydney; the writer is obviously a resident of Sydney, so it is very important to him or her that this passage prove Sydney's greatness. The words "small importance" fit nicely into the paraphrased sentence: "Our goal, in writing this, is one of no small importance, and we believe that every Australian…will wish us good luck" (E). There is no reason for the author to refute the accusation of "evil intent" (A). "Unhappy time" does not make sense in the sentence (B). "Average length" is too literal a translation (C), and the goal of the work is not "description" (D).
13	B	The first paragraph tells the goals of the passage. The second paragraph relates the history of the colonization of Australia, and the third paragraph describes the city of Sydney (B). Although paragraph one does address the reader, paragraph two is not argumentative, and paragraph three is not a summary (A). The paragraphs are not one long narrative (C). Paragraph one is not particularly descriptive, paragraph two is indeed historical, but paragraph three does not tell a story (D). The tone of the passage does not change (E).
14	C	The first sentence of the paragraph says that because the United States rebelled, Britain had to send its convicts elsewhere, implying that previously it had sent its convicts to the U.S. (C). Although Botany Bay was unsuitable, Manly Beach was very suitable for habitation (because Sydney was erected there) (A). There is no evidence that Captain Phillip was not backed by the government (B). Australia had obviously been previously visited as Captain Cook had made a map, which Captain Phillip carried (D). The passage does not state that anyone lived on Manly Beach (E).
15	D	The passage says that even "vessels of the heaviest burden can safely approach the wharves," which means that the harbor must be deep for heavy boats to be able to sail there (D). Religious buildings are mentioned in line 14 (A). The streets "are crossed at right angles," so they are perpendicular (B). Sydney is "unrivaled" in its three-mile coastline (C). The climate is "healthy and dry" (E).

Question	Answer	Explanation
16	A	The sentence boils down to "first you think it's too 'homogenous' but 'you get used to it.'" This is closest to (A). The sentence does not suggest that you "stop noticing" the difference between Australia and England (B). The author does not suggest that people grow to "love" the city (C). Sydney does not seem similar to London (D). The author does not say that people will regret visiting Sydney (E).
17	C	The author raves about the right-angled streets, and calls England's windy streets "undesirable," so he or she would support urban planning (C). The author is confident that "every Australian. . .will heartily bid us 'God speed!'" so he believes he has the full support of Australia (A). Although the author compares Sydney to London, he or she does not say which is better (B). There is no indication of what the author's native land is (D). The author does not find Sydney quaint, but rather progressive. "Gas-lit Streets" and "sumptuous Shops" were not quaint in 1848, when this text was written (E).
18	E	Adrian is "sav'd . . . a day's journey" by the meeting, so it is "fortuitous" (lucky) (E). There is nothing particularly heartwarming about the meeting of spies (A), nor is there any notion of melodrama (B). The men are friendly; there is nothing "acrimonious" (C). We don't know enough about the passage/play to judge it "scandalous" or "surprising" (D).
19	A	This is a good example of picking the least worst answer. "My services are, as you are, against 'em" (lines 4–5) proves that Nicanor is a spy, but all of the other answers are easily proved false (A). There is no mention of a family relationship or of a woman, eliminating (B) and (C). Nicanor is not looking for Coriolanus (D). The two men are friendly; they are not enemies (E).
20	D	"The people against the senators, patricians, and nobles" (lines 15–16) shows that (D) is the correct answer. There is no foreign invasion (A), the military is not overthrowing the government (B), and there is no mention of a royal family (C). A fire is not an insurrection (E).
21	B	The nobles "receive to heart the banishment," so they are not happy about it (B). There is no evidence that the banishment is the cause of the insurrection (A). There is nothing to tell us what role Coriolanus played in the government (C). The men do not support Coriolanus; they are using his absence to their advantage (D). The men are plotting war, so they do not dread it (E).
22	E	"The main blaze" is the people's revolt (E). The insurrection is not quite over: "a small thing would make it flame again" (line 21–22) (A). It can be inferred that the public wanted Coriolanus banished (B). There is no evidence that the flames refer to purgatory (C) or to comments (D).

Question	Answer	Explanation
23	C	The nobles are so mad about Coriolanus, according to the men, that they are about to dissolve the government (lines 23–27) (C). There is no evidence of a romantic entanglement (A). They are not planning to burn the Roman towns (B). The ready army is a plus, but the plan can be hatched without it (D). There is no evidence that the nobles are not ready for war (E).
24	A	Adrian means to say that he is glad to have met Nicador (A). There is no notion of rivalry between the men (B), nor is one making fun of the other (C). There is no mention of any present (D). The men just met; it can't be a cherished friendship (E).
25	D	It's hard to tell much from this short passage, but it's about two men planning a war, so it's most likely historical (D). There's nothing particularly funny (A), nor is it allegorical (B). It doesn't take place in the country (C), and there is nothing that makes it satirical (E).
26	C	Without "his great opposer" Tullus will probably win (C). We do not know if he will do the fighting (A). "Appear" does not refer to his dress (B). There is no evidence that says he'll be required to argue (D) or that he'll need to pretend to be healthy (E).
27	C	The scene's primary purpose is an exchange of information (C). There is no romance mentioned, and there is no comic relief, eliminating (A) and (B). We can't know the audience's interests (D). The passage provides little information on ancient Rome (E).
28	D	Waves do break, so this is not a case of personification (assigning human characteristics to inhuman objects) (D). Life does not really have a "grasp" (A), and it cannot bruise (B). Waves do not clash (C). Armies don't have a "tread" (individual soldiers do) (E).
29	C	The imagery in the first stanza is of "midday" (line 5) while the second stanza speaks of "night" (line 18). Neither stanza speaks of memory (A). Slumber is a metaphor for death, so both stanzas are about death (B). Stanza two is not about the past (D). Patience and hurry are not mentioned in the poem (E).
30	B	Time is compared to "an army's tread" using "as" (B). There are no similes in (A), (C), or (D). Because there is a simile, (E) cannot be correct.
31	D	"Sleep," the title action, is a symbol for death (D). Sleep cannot be a symbol for slumber because the two words mean the same thing (A). It is not a symbol for burial (B). There are no angels in the poem (C). Sleep represents death, not old age (E).
32	B	The author describes life using the words "joy" and "tears" and mentions "a few short years," so (B) is correct. There is no sense in the poem that death creates freedom (A). The author enjoys parts of life, so (C) is too extreme, as is (D). The poem does not contemplate the meaning of life (E).

Question	Answer	Explanation
33	B	The author says that the dead cannot hear and are not harmed by time; death is like sleep, so it is like unconsciousness (B). The author does not only describe life as cruel (A). He does not compare death to being swept away by waves (C). He does not compare different kinds of death (D). Tears are not described as ridiculous (E).
34	A	The author addresses the poem to someone who has died, so it is safe to assume it is written by someone who is grieving (A). Although the author uses "we," he means the human race, not a specific "we" (B). There is no evidence that the author is dying (C). The author describes death as peaceful, so he does not fear it (D). We cannot know if the author has been previously touched by death (E).
35	E	There is no afterlife suggested in the poem (E). (A) is mentioned in lines 3, 4, and 15. (B) is mentioned in lines 6 and 20. Time is compared to an ocean in lines 8–9 (C), and (D) is suggested in line 16.
36	A	The line "when all is touched and tried" (line 17) means "when life has been fully lived" (A). It does not refer to intensity (B) or justice (C). There is no discussion of eternal life in the poem (D). The lines refer to the end of life, not whether it is fruitless (E).
37	D	The action takes place in a country other than China (China is referred to as the "old country"). There is an American girl and electric lights, so (D) is the correct answer, eliminating (A), (B), (C), and (E).
38	A	The author is quoting Yen Chow without using quotation marks, so it is an example of indirect dialogue (A). The author does not intrude in the story (B), and there is no symbolism (C). The character does not change (D), and there is no reference to another literary work (E).
39	C	"There has been silence between them for so long" (lines 42–43) proves that Ming Hoan has not been in contact (C). There is no evidence that Ah Leen has disobeyed her father (A). Although money is mentioned, it is not Yen Chow's only concern (the affront to his family is in his mind) (B). There is no evidence that Ah Leen's American friend has stolen her lover or that Ah Leen is jealous of her, so eliminate (D) and (E).
40	B	The slight is an affront that a divorce will remedy, and Ah Leen's mother says her lover has forgotten her and had a child with another woman, so (B) is the correct answer. The divorce is the remedy, not the insult (A). There is no evidence of an interracial marriage (C). A divorce would be the deviation from custom; it hasn't occurred (D). No elders have been disrespected (E).
41	E	Ah Leen says that they can send her lover away, but they can't make her love anyone else (E). The perfume is a symbol of love, not marriage (A). Perfume does not symbolize time (B) or the marriage bond (C). It does not represent mutual love (D).

Question	Answer	Explanation
42	A	At first the reader is inside Yen Chow's head; then the reader is inside the American girl's head, so it is a change in point of view (A). The kind of words the author uses does not change (B). There is no time change (C). The characters' dialogue is uniform (D), and there is no change in theme (E).
43	A	"Like a pale yellow pearl" (line 32) is a simile (A). Nothing is given human characteristics, so eliminate (B) and (E). There is no example of alliteration (C), and nothing is particularly parallel (D).
44	D	The girl keeps repeating the words and wants to send a message to someone; it has obviously made her rethink a relationship (D). There is no evidence that the American girl even knows Ming Hoan's parents (A) or that she has a history with Ming Hoan (B). The girl does not take offense (C). The girl does not repeat his words in incomprehension (E).
45	C	Ming Hoan does not explain because "the sins of parents must not be uncovered" (lines 41–42) (C). It is not because he is afraid of hurting his love (A) or that he is embarrassed (B). There is no evidence that he doesn't feel he needs to explain (D), and the fact that she doesn't ask is not the reason the story gives (E).
46	B	Ah Leen says in lines 37–39, "Though another had bound you by human ties, to me you were linked by my love divine" (B). There is no preference for old customs (A). There is no evidence that true love cannot be extinguished (C). There is no evidence that their love has grown (D) or that the heart of another is unknowable (E).
47	E	The words are parallel to "ruined by rain," so the answer must be equally as destructive (E). (A) and (B) are not strong enough, while (C) and (D) have the opposite meaning the poem intends.
48	B	The poet is in "pain" and expresses "hate," so he is stung (B). His words are much too bitter for him to be resigned (A). He is not sulking (C). He is not "inured" (accustomed) (D), nor is he "imperious" (arrogant) (E).
49	E	There are no exotic images, and the poet does not appear to dream (E). Water appears in line 12 (A). Many plants appear: "rose," "fruit," etc. Eliminate (B). Wine appears in line 22 (C), and melody is referred to in line 10 (D).
50	B	"Smitten with sunbeams, ruined with rain" are examples of alliteration (A). There are no religious images in the first stanza (B). The author does not preach (C). He is not antipathetic (D), and character is not really revealed (the poem is more about emotions in general than in this poet's specific feelings) (E).
51	C	The poem is about how he has lost his love, and music is what he now hates (C). Death is not a theme in the poem (A). Music and fruit are both symbols, but the poet does not compare music to fruit (B). There is no mention of original sin in the poem (D), and the poet does not talk about slyness or snakes (E).
52	B	These are not human characteristics given to inhuman objects (B). Personification is present in (A) ("singing seasons"), (C) ("heavens that murmur"), (D) ("stars that sing"), and (E) ("music burning").

Question	Answer	Explanation
53	E	These "things are over" (line 26) according to the author, so they are examples of how love feels. There are no anecdotes (A). The memories are not necessarily unpleasant (B). The stanza does not literally speak of weather (C). Fate is not a part of the poem (E).
54	D	The eighth line must rhyme with the second and third lines and lament the loss of love (D). (A) and (B) do not rhyme with the correct lines. (C) does not make sense in the context; day and night are not mentioned in the poem. (E) is incorrect, as the poet never mentions the wish for head and heart to mingle.
55	B	The men disagree on music, and Nanapush is teaching his language to Father Damien, so (B) is the correct answer. There is no evidence that they are old friends (A). We cannot predict the future, and there is nothing to suggest the men don't get along (C). They are not negotiators (D). Only Father Damien is clearly part of a church (E).
56	C	The first paragraph is reported dialogue, while the rest of the passage is quoted dialogue (C). The future is never discussed (A). There is no movement from general to specific or from complexity to simplicity, so eliminate (D) and (E). No one recites or utters a soliloquy (D).
57	E	The word is a sound of surprise and understanding, an interjection (E). It is not singing (A). Father Damien speaks English; this word is not English (B). It does not try to mimic the sound of Chopin (C). It is not Father Damien's first name (D).
58	E	Music's influence is discussed throughout the passage (E). The cultural differences exist, but are not the main theme of the passage (A). There is no ironic subtext (B). Although Nanapush uses music to pursue women, this is not the main theme of the passage (C), nor are relationships (D).
59	A	Nanapush asks many questions, so (A) is the correct answer. He does not patronize Father Damien—in fact, he asks him questions (B). He is not overly guarded or polite (C). He is not "kissing up to" Father Damien (D). And his passion is not clearly scholarly (E).
60	C	Father Damien is describing the emotion he feels when he hears Chopin (C). The emotion is not necessarily joy ("Dogs cry," line 28) (A). There is no sense of nostalgia mentioned (B). (D) is too literal an answer. Although "you can't think," "flooded in the heart" is more of an infusion of emotion than confusion (E).
61	C	The image of the piano sitting in the river bed while the river rushes around it shows that Father Damien considers time eternal and that the piano (i.e., music) is, too (C). The men are speaking in English (A). He does not think that wood is too common a material; he even calls it "precious." (B). The image of the piano is foremost in his mind, but it is not the reason he says the piano is made of "time" (D). There is no evidence that he feels uncomfortable with the topic (E).

Chapter 19
Practice Test 4

PRACTICE SAT LITERATURE
SUBJECT TEST 4

LITERATURE TEST 4

Directions: This test consists of selections from literary works and questions on their content, form, and style. After reading each passage or poem, choose the best answer to each question and fill in the corresponding oval on the answer sheet.

Note: Pay particular attention to questions that contain the words NOT, LEAST, or EXCEPT.

Questions 1-9. Read the following passage carefully before you choose your answers.

While they had been young, no event in the
social world of Elsinore had been a success
without the lovely De Coninck sisters. They were
the heart and soul of all the gayety of the town.
5   When they entered its ballrooms, the ceilings of
sedate old merchants' houses seemed to lift a little,
and the walls to spring out in luminous Ionian
columns, bound with vine. When one of them
opened the ball, light as a bird, bold as a thought,
10   she consecrated the gathering to the gods of true
joy of life, from whose presence care and envy
are banished. They could sing duets like a pair of
nightingales in a tree, and imitate without effort
and without the slightest malice the voices of all
15   the *beau monde* of Elsinore, so as to make the
paunches of their father's friends, the matadors of
the town, shake with laughter around their card
tables. They could make up a charade or a game
of forfeits in no time, and when they had been out
20   for their music lessons, or to the Promenade, they
came back brimful of tales of what had happened,
or of tales out of their own imaginations, one whim
stumbling over the other.
   And then, within their own rooms, they would
25   walk up and down the floor and weep, or sit in the
window and look out over the harbor and wring
their hands in their laps, or lie in bed at night
and cry bitterly, for no reason in the world. They
would talk, then, of life with the black bitterness of
30   two Timons of Athens, and give Madam Baek an
uncanny feeling, as in an atmosphere of corrodent
rust. Their mother, who did not have the curse in
her blood, would have been badly frightened had
she been present at these moments, and would have
35   suspected some unhappy love affair. Their father
would have understood them, and have grieved on
their behalf, but he was occupied with his affairs,
and did not come into his daughters' rooms. Only
this elderly female servant, whose temperament
40   was as different as possible from theirs, would
understand them in her way, and would keep
it all within her heart, as they did themselves,
with mingled despair and pride. Sometimes she
would try to comfort them. When they cried out,
45   "Hanne, is it not terrible that there is so much
lying, so much falsehood, in the world?" she said,
"Well, what of it? It would be worse still if it were
actually true, all that they tell."
   Then again the girls would get up, dry their
50   tears, try on their new bonnets before the glass,
plan their theatricals and sleighing parties, shock
and gladden the hearts of their friends, and have
the whole thing over again. They seemed as unable
to keep from one extremity as from the other.
55   In short, they were born melancholiacs, such as
make others happy and are themselves helplessly
unhappy, creatures of playfulness, charm and salt
tears, of fine fun and everlasting loneliness.

(1934)

1. Which of the following is personified in the first paragraph of the passage (lines 1-23) ?

   (A) Voices
   (B) Nightingales
   (C) Walls
   (D) Paunches
   (E) Ballrooms

2. The sisters can best be described as

   (A) vivacious yet standoffish
   (B) joyful yet impolite
   (C) beloved yet acrimonious
   (D) popular yet superficial
   (E) amusing yet despairing

3. The "curse in her blood" (lines 32-33) refers to

   (A) bad luck in romance
   (B) the strain of melancholy inherited by the sisters
   (C) the mother's lack of talent
   (D) the girls' overreaction to events
   (E) the mother's constant fear

GO ON TO THE NEXT PAGE

4. The style of the last line can best be described as

   (A) a description of contrasts
   (B) an extended analogy
   (C) authorial intrusion
   (D) ironic detachment
   (E) subtle differentiation

5. In contrast to the sisters, Hanne is

   (A) practical
   (B) reassuring
   (C) dismissive
   (D) uncaring
   (E) even-tempered

6. The sentence "When one of them opened the ball, light as a bird, bold as a thought, she consecrated the gathering to the gods of true joy of life, from whose presence care and envy are banished" (lines 8-12) can best be restated as

   (A) the sisters acted as religious figures, blessing events
   (B) the sisters were anxious hosts, making sure their guests were enjoying themselves
   (C) if the sisters were at the ball, it could be considered a success
   (D) the sisters were so delightful that everyone in their presence had a good time
   (E) the girls never worried about or were jealous of others

7. Which of the following is NOT mentioned as a talent of the sisters?

   (A) storytelling
   (B) singing
   (C) impersonations
   (D) organizing games
   (E) decorating

8. In this context, "uncanny" (line 31) most nearly means

   (A) concerned
   (B) uncomfortable
   (C) preoccupied
   (D) poisonous
   (E) invigorating

9. It can be inferred from the passage that the sisters

   (A) were members of the upper class
   (B) suffered from crippling clinical depression
   (C) were in search of appropriate husbands
   (D) were easily frightened
   (E) were indifferent to male attention

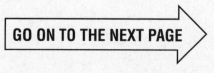

GO ON TO THE NEXT PAGE

Questions 10-18. Read the following passage carefully before you choose your answers.

In the second year of the reign of Valentinian and Valens, on the morning of the twenty-first day of July, the greatest part of the Roman world was shaken by a violent and destructive earthquake.

The impression was communicated to the waters; the shores of the Mediterranean were left dry, by the sudden retreat of the sea; great quantities of fish were caught with the hand;
5 large vessels were stranded on the mud; and a curious spectator amused his eye, or rather his fancy, by contemplating the various appearance of valleys and mountains, which had never, since the formation of the globe, been exposed to the
10 sun. But the tide soon returned, with the weight of an immense and irresistible deluge, which was severely felt on the coasts of Sicily, of Dalmatia, of Greece, and of Egypt: large boats were transported, and lodged on the roofs of houses,
15 or at the distance of two miles from the shore; the people, with their habitations, were swept away by the waters; and the city of Alexandria annually commemorated the fatal day, on which fifty thousand persons had lost their lives in the
20 inundation.
    This calamity, the report of which was magnified from one province to another, astonished and terrified the subjects of Rome; and their affrighted imagination enlarged the real extent of
25 a momentary evil. They recollected the preceding earthquakes, which had subverted the cities of Palestine and Bithynia: they considered these alarming strokes as the prelude only of still more dreadful calamities, and their fearful vanity was
30 disposed to confound the symptoms of a declining empire and a sinking world.

(1776)

10. Which of the following is NOT a result of the earthquake?

(A) beached vessels
(B) scorched earth
(C) extensive property damage
(D) many casualties
(E) widespread flooding

11. The sentence "the impression was communicated to the waters" (lines 1-2) most nearly means

(A) citizens sent distress signals via boats
(B) the water carried the sound of the earthquake
(C) the earthquake took place off shore
(D) the earthquake caused water displacement
(E) the sea parted with the power of the earthquake

12. It can be inferred from the passage that Rome's citizens

(A) had never before seen such widespread destruction
(B) placed a great deal of value on human life
(C) thought the world was deteriortating
(D) understood the causes of natural disasters
(E) were not prone to confabulation

13. The author's tone can best be described as

(A) detached
(B) disparaging
(C) amused
(D) frightened
(E) alarmist

14. It can be inferred from the passage that people affected by the earthquake were

(A) homogenous
(B) superstitious
(C) reactionary
(D) insightful
(D) regretful

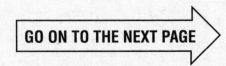

GO ON TO THE NEXT PAGE

15. Which of the following quotes best describes the reason the Romans were so frightened by the earthquake?

    (A) "they considered these alarming strokes as the prelude only of still more dreadful calamities"(lines 27-29)
    (B) "the city of Alexandria annually commemorated the fatal day, on which fifty thousand persons had lost their lives in the inundation" (lines 17-20)
    (C) "a curious spectator amused his eye, or rather his fancy, by contemplating the various appearance of valleys and mountains, which had never, since the formation of the globe, been exposed to the sun" (lines 5-10)
    (D) "They recollected the preceding earthquakes, which had subverted the cities of Palestine and Bithynia" (lines 25-27)
    (E) "But the tide soon returned, with the weight of an immense and irresistible deluge, which was severely felt" (lines 10-12)

16. In context, "declining" most nearly means

    (A) sinking
    (B) worsening
    (C) aging
    (D) shrinking
    (E) weary

17. Which of the following is true, according to the passage?

    (A) The Roman Empire lost 50,000 people.
    (B) Homes were destroyed by the rift in the earth.
    (C) The earthquakes in Bithnyia and Palestine were not as destructive as this earthquake.
    (D) The Mediterranean's tides were permanently affected.
    (E) The damage was primarily caused by a surge of water.

18. The following three lines all contain

    I. "the people, with their habitations, were swept away by the waters" (lines 16-17)
    II. "great quantities of fish were caught with the hand" (lines 3-4)
    III. "The impression was communicated to the waters" (lines 1-2)
    (A) figurative language
    (B) colorful adjectives
    (C) passive verb construction
    (D) oxymoronic impossibilities
    (E) pastoral analogies

GO ON TO THE NEXT PAGE

Questions 19-28. Read the following poem carefully before you choose your answers.

"To my Honoured Kinsman John Driden, of Chesterton, in the County of Huntingdon, Esq."

How blessed is he, who leads a country life,
Unvexed with anxious cares, and void of strife!
Who, studying peace, and shunning civil rage,
Enjoyed his youth, and now enjoys his age:
5 All who deserve his love, he makes his own;
And, to be loved himself, needs only to be known.
Just, good, and wise, contending neighbors come,
From your award to wait their final doom;
And, foes before, return in friendship home
10 Without their cost, you terminate the cause,
And save the expense of long litigious laws;
Where suits are traversed, and so little won,
That he who conquers is but last undone:
Such are not your decrees; but so designed,
15 The sanction leaves a lasting peace behind;
Like your own soul, serene, a pattern of your mind.
Promoting concord, and composing strife,
Lord of yourself, uncumbered with a wife;
Where, for a year, a month, perhaps a night,
20 Long penitence succeeds a short delight:
Minds are so hardly matched, that even the first,
Though paired by heaven, in Paradise were cursed.

(1697)

19. In context "void of" (line 2) most nearly means

(A) empty of
(B) lacking
(C) reversed in
(D) canceled from
(E) disqualified for

20. The last two lines refer to

(A) the poet and his wife
(B) the subject of the poem and his mistress
(C) Adam and Eve
(D) Romeo and Juliet
(E) a hypothetical pair of lovers

21. It can be inferred from the poem that the poet considers country life to be

(A) tedious
(B) onerous
(C) momentous
(D) undesirable
(E) idyllic

22. Which of the following is NOT mentioned by the poet as a benefit of country living?

(A) a calm mind
(B) old age
(C) many friends
(D) wisdom
(E) good health

23. It can be inferred from the poem that the author thinks of marriage as

(A) a necessary evil
(B) an unavoidable concession
(C) a protracted lawsuit
(D) a source of aggravation
(E) a prison sentence

GO ON TO THE NEXT PAGE

24. Which of the following best describes the difference between lines 1-6 and lines 7-22?

    (A) generalization to direct address
    (B) present tense to past tense
    (C) positive discourse to negative discourse
    (D) simple description to extended simile
    (E) terrestrial presence to divine intervention

25. The word "their" (line 8) refers to

    (A) suits
    (B) expenses
    (C) foes
    (D) neighbors
    (E) laws

26. Which of the following best describes the subject of the poem's role in his community?

    (A) farmer
    (B) judge
    (C) religious leader
    (D) writer
    (E) scholar

27. Which of the following contains an example of alliteration?

    I. "And, foes before, return in friendship home" (line 9)
    II. "And save the expense of long litigious laws" (line 11)
    III. "Long penitence succeeds a short delight" (line 20)

    (A) I only
    (B) II only
    (C) III only
    (D) I and III only
    (E) I, II, and III

28. Lines 21-22 can be restated as

    (A) True equality is hard to come by; and whenever it does occur, it is cursed by God.
    (B) It's difficult to get along with someone else; even God's original creations fought.
    (C) The more alike two people are, the more they're prone to argue.
    (D) Soul mates are rare; the rest of humanity lives outside Paradise with incompatible spouses.
    (E) It is wise to disguise intelligence—those who are exceptional are often cast out of society.

GO ON TO THE NEXT PAGE

Questions 29-36. Read the following poem carefully before you choose your answers.

"To My Own Soul"

Hold yet a while, Strong Heart,
Not part a lifelong yoke
Though blighted looks the present, future gloom.
And age it seems since you and I began our
5 March up hill or down. Sailing smooth o'er
Seas that are so rare—
Thou nearer unto me, than oft-times I myself—
Proclaiming mental moves before they were!
Reflector true—Thy pulse so timed to mine,
10 Thou perfect note of thoughts, however fine—
Shall we now part, Recorder, say?
In thee is friendship, faith,
For thou didst warn when evil thoughts were brewing—
15 And though, alas, thy warning thrown away,
Went on the same as ever—good and true.

(1847)

29. In the poem, the speaker uses all of the following to replace the subject of his address EXCEPT

(A) thou
(B) reflector
(C) recorder
(D) heart
(E) faith

30. In this context "brewing" most nearly means

(A) threatening
(B) forming
(C) clouding
(D) imbibing
(E) foreshadowing

31. It is clear from the first three lines that the poet regards his heart as

(A) aching for the love of another
(B) failing and ceasing to function
(C) a separate entity
(D) wanting to separate from his body
(E) an enemy of his soul

32. The lines "And age it seems since you and I began our March up hill or down. Sailing smooth o'er Seas that are so rare—" can best be restated as

(A) "We've been through many travails, some easy, some more difficult."
(B) "Our journey will take a long while and range over land and sea."
(C) "We are prisoners of an army from across the ocean."
(D) "It is unfortunate that most of our journey has not been on the water."
(E) "We are now too old to hike; sailing is easier on our frail limbs."

33. All of the following are themes of the poem EXCEPT

(A) love
(B) loyalty
(C) faith
(D) morality
(E) time

34. The author employs which of the following unusual techniques:

I. punctuation functioning as words
II. rhythm reflecting theme
III. form mirroring content

(A) I only
(B) III only
(C) I and II
(D) I and III
(E) I, II, and III

35. The poet's tone can best be described as

(A) despairing
(B) grateful
(C) resigned
(D) proud
(E) questioning

36. "Thou perfect note of thoughts" (line 10) is an example of

(A) alliteration
(B) personification
(C) metaphor
(D) paradox
(E) allegory

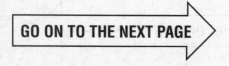
GO ON TO THE NEXT PAGE

Questions 37-44. Read the following passage carefully before you choose your answers.

Eugene Coristine and Farquhar Wilkinson were youngish bachelors and fellow members of the Victoria and Albert Literary Society. Thither, on
5 Wednesday evenings, when respectable church-members were wending their way to weekly service, they hastened regularly, to meet with a band of like-minded young men, and spend a literary hour or two. In various degrees of fluency they debated the questions of the day; they read
10 essays with a wide range of style and topic; they gave readings from popular authors, and contributed airy creations in prose and in verse to the Society's manuscript magazine. Wilkinson, the older and more sedate of the two, who wore a
15 tightly-buttoned blue frock coat and an eyeglass, was a schoolmaster, pretty well up in the Toronto Public Schools. Coristine was a lawyer in full practice, but his name did not appear on the card of the firm which profited by his services. He was
20 taller than his friend, more jauntily dressed, and was of a more mercurial temperament than the schoolmaster, for whom, however, he entertained a profound respect. Different as they were, they were linked together by an ardent love of literature,
25 especially poetry, by scientific pursuits, Coristine as a botanist, and Wilkinson as a dabbler in geology, and by a firm determination to resist, or rather to shun, the allurements of female society. Many lady teachers wielded the pointer in rooms
30 not far removed from those in which Mr. Wilkinson held sway, but he did not condescend to be on terms even of bowing acquaintance with any one of them. There were several young lady typewriters of respectable city connections in the offices of
35 Messrs. Tyler, Woodruff and White, but the young Irish lawyer passed them by without a glance. These bachelors were of the opinion that women were bringing the dignity of law and education to the dogs.

(1892)

37. The two men have all of the following in common EXCEPT

(A) they are both unmarried
(B) they both look down upon women
(C) they are both professionals
(D) they are both bibliophiles
(E) they both speak foreign languages

38. The phrase "well up" (line 16) in this context most nearly means

(A) handsomely paid
(B) generally liked
(C) professionally advanced
(D) comfortably sated
(E) nattily dressed

39. The sentence "Thither, on Wednesday evenings, when respectable church-members were wending their way to weekly service, they hastened regularly, to meet with a band of like-minded young men, and spend a literary hour or two" (lines 3-8) suggests the men are

(A) chauvinists
(B) talented authors
(C) lapsed church-members
(D) dishonorable
(E) pious

40. In this context, "mercurial" (line 21) most nearly means

(A) excitable
(B) overheated
(C) incorrigible
(D) embarrassed
(E) self-confident

41. From the passage it is reasonable to conclude that the two men

(A) had little opportunity to meet women
(B) felt threatened by female influence
(C) feared their jobs would be taken by women
(D) considered women generally inferior to men
(E) felt that women were fit only for teaching and clerical work

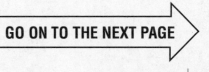
GO ON TO THE NEXT PAGE

42. By the phrase, "Coristine was a lawyer in full
    practice, but his name did not appear on the card
    of the firm which profited by his services" the
    author suggests that

    (A) Coristine is not valued by his firm
    (B) Coristine does not have enough money to have
        business cards made
    (C) although he was part of a firm, he worked
        independently
    (D) Coristine did not contribute sufficiently to his
        company's earnings
    (E) Coristine is at the beginning of his career

43. The tone of the passage can best be described as

    (A) indignantly offended
    (B) gently mocking
    (C) hesitantly critical
    (D) unflinchingly honest
    (E) offhandedly distant

44. As it is used in the passage, the phrase "wending
    their way" (line 5) can best be replaced with the
    words

    (A) journeying to
    (B) hastening to
    (C) retiring from
    (D) returning from
    (E) late to

Questions 45-53. Read the following poem carefully before you choose your answers.

"The City Heiress"

How vain have prov'd the Labours of the Stage,
In striving to reclaim a vitious Age!
Poets may write the Mischief to impeach,
You care as little what the Poets teach,
5   As you regard at Church what Parsons preach.
But where such Follies, and such Vices reign,
What honest Pen has Patience to refrain?
At Church, in Pews, ye most devoutly snore;
And here, got dully drunk, ye come to roar:
10   Ye go to Church to glout*, and ogle there,
And come to meet more leud convenient here

With equal Zeal ye honour either Place,
And run so very evenly your Race,
Y' improve in Wit just as you do in Grace
15   It must be so, some Doemon** has possest
Our Land, and we have never since been blest.

    *to pout or look sullen
    **demon

                           (1682)

45. In this context, "vain" (line 1) most nearly means

  (A) boastful
  (B) desperate
  (C) wasted
  (D) capricious
  (E) complex

46. The first two lines "How vain have prov'd the Labours of the Stage, In striving to reclaim a vitious Age!" suggest that

  (A) the speaker considers actors a self-important group
  (B) the speaker considers the theater world to be full of back-stabbing heathens
  (C) the speaker considers that the theater's attempt to improve society's morality has failed
  (D) acting requires more work than most common citizens understand
  (E) through good theater, people can be metaphorically transported back in time

47. Which of the following is an example of personification?

  (A) "Poets may write the Mischief to impeach" (line 3)
  (B) "What honest Pen has Patience to refrain?" (line 7)
  (C) "And run so very evenly your Race" (line 13)
  (D) "Y' improve in Wit just as you do in Grace" (line 14)
  (E) "It must be so, some Doemon has possest" (line 15)

48. The poem consists of

  (A) arrhythmic rhyme
  (B) rhyming couplets only
  (C) rhyming couplets and triplets
  (D) epic hyperbole
  (E) passive verbs only

49. From the poem, it is reasonable to infer that the speaker regards the church as

  (A) intensely boring
  (B) ineffective in its teachings
  (C) a den of gossip
  (D) the domain of hypocrites
  (E) inferior to theater

50. The tone of lines 13-14, "And run so very evenly your Race,/Y' improve in Wit just as you do in Grace," can best be described as

  (A) hyperbolic
  (B) sarcastic
  (C) condemning
  (D) admiring
  (E) parodical

51. According to the poet, people do all of the following in church and/or the theater EXCEPT

  (A) look at others
  (B) nap soundly
  (C) heckle the stage
  (D) conduct contests
  (E) become inebriated

GO ON TO THE NEXT PAGE

52. Which of the following phrases has the same narrative effect as "devoutly snore" (line 8) ?

   (A) Loudly read
   (B) Hatefully praise
   (C) Awkwardly leap
   (D) Forwardly slide
   (E) Piously stand

53. Why does line 14 "Y' improve in Wit just as you do in Grace" contain an abbreviation?

   (A) In the seventeenth century "you" or "ye" was commonly spelled "y."
   (B) Because the poet wrote in longhand, the abbreviation was an attempt to save copying time.
   (C) To form alliteration with "your" (line 13) and "you" (line 14).
   (D) To make the line fit the poem's meter.
   (E) To make it evident that a new subject is being addressed.

Questions 54-62. Read the following passage carefully before you choose your answers.

In the mind of the mariner, there is a superstitious horror connected with the name of Pirate; and there are few subjects that interest and excite the curiosity of mankind generally,
5 more than the desperate exploits, foul doings, and diabolical career of these monsters in human form. A piratical crew is generally formed of the desperadoes and runagates of every clime and nation. The pirate, from the perilous nature of his
10 occupation, when not cruising on the ocean, the great highway of nations, selects the most lonely isles of the sea for his retreat, or secretes himself near the shores of rivers, bays and lagoons of thickly wooded and uninhabited countries, so
15 that if pursued he can escape to the woods and mountain glens of the interior. The islands of the Indian Ocean, and the east and west coasts of Africa, as well as the West Indies, have been their haunts for centuries; and vessels navigating the
20 Atlantic and Indian Oceans, are often captured by them, the passengers and crew murdered, the money and most valuable part of the cargo plundered, the vessel destroyed, thus obliterating all trace of their unhappy fate, and leaving
25 friends and relatives to mourn their loss from the inclemencies of the elements, when they were butchered in cold blood by their fellow men, who by practically adopting the maxim that "dead men tell no tales," enable themselves to pursue their
30 diabolical career with impunity....

But the apprehension and foreboding of the mind, when under the influence of remorse, are powerful, and every man, whether civilized or savage, has interwoven in his constitution a moral
35 sense, which secretly condemns him when he has committed an atrocious action, even when he is placed in situations which raise him above the fear of human punishment, for "Conscience, the torturer of the soul, unseen. Does fiercely brandish
40 a sharp scourge within; Severe decrees may keep our tongues in awe, but to our minds what edicts can give law? Even you yourself to your own breast shall tell Your crimes, and your own conscience be your hell."

(1837)

GO ON TO THE NEXT PAGE

54. Which of the following sentences best describes the passage's structure?

    (A) Paragraph one introduces a topic, while paragraph two further elaborates, citing poetic evidence.
    (B) Paragraph one states a point of view, while paragraph two opposes it.
    (C) Paragraph one states the general perception of a profession, while paragraph two delves into the actual emotions of the individuals in that profession.
    (D) Paragraph one explains atrocities, and paragraph two justifies them.
    (E) Paragraph one provides background on a topic, while paragraph two gives a contemporary popular culture example.

55. Which of the following situations would be most analogous to the author's suppositions about pirates' emotions?

    (A) A student who cheated on a test but felt so bad about it that he turned himself in
    (B) A student who cheated on a test and gave her transgression no more than a passing thought
    (C) A student who falsely accused another student of cheating, and then retracted his statement because of guilt
    (D) A student who cheated on a test but felt so ashamed that he was unable to enjoy the high grade he received
    (E) A student who cheated on a test but felt justified in doing so because the teacher had not properly prepared her for the material on the test

56. Which of the following is an example of a metaphor?

    (A) "their haunts for centuries" (lines 18-19)
    (B) "the desperate exploits, foul doings, and diabolical career" (lines 5-6)
    (C) "the great highway of nations" (lines 10-11)
    (D) "the desperadoes and runagates of every clime and nation" (lines 7-9)
    (E) "the apprehension and foreboding of the mind" (lines 31-32)

57. The author's prose can be characterized as

    (A) descriptively complex, using extensive modifiers and subordinate clauses
    (B) deceptively ornate, couching a simple subject in complicated language
    (C) rhetorically interrogative, raising questions that the author never answers
    (D) narrowly biased, providing a unilateral viewpoint
    (E) defensively argumentative, anticipating critical objections and rejecting them

58. The word "secretes" as it is used in the passage most nearly means

    (A) admits
    (B) ensconces
    (C) emanates
    (D) disguises
    (E) silences

59. According to the passage, what do relatives of the victims believe happened to the victims?

    (A) They died of scurvy or other shipborne diseases.
    (B) They were murdered by pirates.
    (C) They were kidnapped by foreign cultures to be sold as slaves.
    (D) They succumbed to the lure of the open ocean.
    (E) They capsized in a large storm and drowned.

60. The author most likely believes in

    (A) a universal conscience that transcends cultures
    (B) a supreme deity who governs all actions
    (C) a higher court to which murderers are held
        accountable
    (D) the potential power of international law
    (E) the importance of nurture in the development
        of a moral code

61. The use of the word "practically" (line 28)

    (A) proves that murderers are always haunted by
        remorse
    (B) suggests that not all victims were killed
    (C) insinuates that the pirates were motivated only
        by greed
    (D) explains the logic behind murder
    (E) implies that the author is not exactly sure of
        the pirates' actions

62. The author inserts the poem/song at the end most
    likely to

    (A) liven up a boring narrative
    (B) prove a point by quoting an expert source
    (C) discuss an opinion in a memorable fashion
    (D) provide a text for subsequent analysis
    (E) appease readers who prefer rhyme to prose

STOP

**IF YOU FINISH BEFORE TIME IS CALLED, YOU MAY CHECK YOUR WORK ON THIS SECTION ONLY.
DO NOT TURN TO ANY OTHER SECTION IN THE TEST.**

How to Score The Princeton Review
Practice SAT Literature Subject Test

When you take the real exam, the proctors will collect your test booklet and bubble sheet and send your answer sheet to New Jersey where a computer looks at the pattern of filled-in ovals on your answer sheet and gives you a score. We couldn't include even a small computer with this book, so we are providing this more primitive way of scoring your exam.

Determining Your Score

STEP 1   Using the answer key on the next page, determine how many questions you got right and how many you got wrong on the test. Remember, questions that you do not answer do not count as either right or wrong answers.

STEP 2   List the number of right answers here.   (A) _____

STEP 3   List the number of wrong answers here. Now divide that   (B) _____ ÷ 4 = (C) _____
number by 4. (Use a calculator if you're feeling particularly lazy.)

STEP 4   Subtract the number of wrong answers divided by 4 from the (A) − (C) = _____
number of correct answers. Round this score to the nearest whole number. This is your raw score.

STEP 5   To determine your real score, take the number from Step 4 and look it up in the left-hand column of the Score Conversion Table on page 231; the corresponding score on the right is your score on the exam.

Answer Key to Practice SAT Literature Subject Test 4

1. C	17. E	33. A	49. B
2. E	18. C	34. A	50. B
3. B	19. B	35. B	51. D
4. A	20. C	36. C	52. B
5. E	21. E	37. E	53. D
6. D	22. E	38. C	54. C
7. E	23. D	39. D	55. D
8. B	24. A	40. A	56. C
9. A	25. D	41. D	57. A
10. B	26. B	42. A	58. B
11. D	27. E	43. B	59. E
12. C	28. B	44. A	60. A
13. B	29. E	45. C	61. D
14. B	30. B	46. C	62. B
15. A	31. D	47. B	
16. B	32. A	48. C	

SAT Literature Subject Test—Score Conversion Table

Raw Score	College Board Scaled Score	Raw Score	College Board Scaled Score
62	800	23	500
61	800	22	490
60	800	21	490
59	800	20	480
58	800	19	470
57	800	18	460
56	800	17	450
55	790	16	440
54	780	15	430
53	780	14	420
52	770	13	410
51	760	12	410
50	750	11	400
49	740	10	390
48	730	09	380
47	720	08	370
46	710	07	360
45	700	06	350
44	700	05	350
43	690	04	340
42	680	03	330
41	670	02	320
40	660	01	310
39	650	00	300
38	640	-01	300
37	630	-02	290
36	620	-03	280
35	620	-04	270
34	610	-05	260
33	600	-06	250
32	590	-07	240
31	580	-08	240
30	570	-09	230
29	560	-10	220
28	550	-11	210
27	540	-12	200
26	530	-13	200
27	540	-14	200
26	530	-15	200
25	520		
24	510		

Chapter 20
Practice Test 4:
Answers and Explanations

Answers and Explanations

Question	Answer	Explanation
1	C	Walls are said to "spring out" (line 7), a human capacity, so that is the example of personification in the first paragraph (C). None of the other answer choices are examples of personification.
2	E	The sisters are said to make their father's friends "shake with laughter" (line 17) but often "weep" (line 25), so they are "amusing yet despairing." They may be "vivacious," but they are not "standoffish" (A). They may be "joyful," but they are not "impolite" (B). They are "beloved" but not "acrimonious" (hostile) (C), and they are not "superficial" (D).
3	B	The curse refers to the melancholy the sisters suffered that their mother did not have (B). There is no evidence that the girls were unlucky in romance (A). The mother's talent (or lack thereof) is not mentioned (C). The "curse" is not the silliness of overreaction to events (D), and the mother's fear is not described as "constant" (E).
4	A	The last sentence describes contrasts: the girls make people happy but they themselves are unhappy; they are fun but are themselves lonely (A). There is no analogy (B). The author does not make an appearance in the passage, nor does the voice change (C). The narrator is not particularly detached (D). The differentiation between "happy" and "sad" is not subtle (E).
5	E	The sisters are prone to wild mood swings, but Hanne's "temperament was as different as possible from theirs" (lines 39–40) (E). There is no evidence that Hanne is "practical," or that the sisters are not (A). Although Hanne attempts to reassure the girls, the girls are not unreassuring (B). Hanne is not "dismissive" (C), nor is she "uncaring" (D).
6	D	The sentence states that the girls were the life of the party (D). The "gods of true joy" do not refer to real religion (A). The sisters are not the hostesses of these parties (B). Although (C) is mentioned in the passage, this sentence does not suggest that the girls' mere presence guaranteed social success. The girls banish "care and envy" but there is no evidence that they themselves were never worried or jealous (E).
7	E	The girls are never described as decorators (E). They are good storytellers: "brimful of tales" (line 21) (A). They sing like "a pair of nightingales" (lines 12–13) (B). They were excellent imitators (line 13) (C), and they could "make up a charade or a game of forfeits" (lines 18–19) (D).
8	B	The girls make Madam Baek feel as though she was in an "atmosphere of rust" (i.e., uncomfortable) (B). Although she may be concerned, this is not the meaning of uncanny (A). Nor is "preoccupied" a good synonym for her feeling of unease (C). Neither "poisonous" (D) nor "invigorating" (E) make sense here.

Question	Answer	Explanation
9	A	The girls are obviously educated in the arts and spend their time at balls and not at work, plus the family has at least one servant, so it is logical to conclude that they are members of the upper class (A). Unless we are their psychiatrists, we can't diagnose their illness, and the narrator doesn't tell us what they suffered from (B). There is no mention of a search for a husband (C). There is no evidence that they were frightened (D) or that they didn't care if men paid them attention or not (E).
10	B	Here you're looking for the thing that is NOT in the passage. Choice (A) is an effect of the earthquake: "large vessels were stranded on the mud" (line 5). Choice (C) is also a result of the earthquake: "the people, with their habitations, were swept away by the waters" (lines 16–17), as is (D), "fifty thousand persons had lost their lives in the inundation" (lines 19–20), and (E) "But the tide soon returned, with the weight of an immense and irresistible deluge, which was severely felt on the coasts of Sicily, of Dalmatia, of Greece, and of Egypt" (lines 10–13). There is no evidence of "scorched earth" (B), as there was no mention of fire.
11	D	The earthquake caused the water first to retreat, and then to flood the coastal areas, so (D) is the correct answer. There is no mention of distress signals (A). The "impression" refers to the physical movement of the water, not of sound (B). We do not know where the quake took place (C). There is no evidence that the sea parted, merely that it retreated and then flooded (E).
12	C	The passage makes clear that Roman citizens thought the world was worsening: "their fearful vanity was disposed to confound the symptoms of a declining empire and a sinking world" (lines 29–31), so (C) is the correct answer. There are two other earthquakes mentioned, Palestine and Bithynia, but the current destruction is not compared to them (A). There is no evidence in the passage that Romans placed a great value on human life (B). There is no evidence that they understood the cause of the earthquake; in fact, they thought it was a sign of a worsening world (D). They *were* prone to confabulation (E); the extent of the destruction was exaggerated: "This calamity, the report of which was magnified from one province to another" (lines 21–22).
13	B	The author speaks of the people's "affrighted imagination" and "fearful vanity" and says they think they brought on the earthquake, so he is not respectful of the Roman people (B). The author is not particularly detached—in fact, he imagines himself at the scene: "a curious spectator amused his eye, or rather his fancy, by contemplating the various appearance of valleys and mountains" (lines 5–8). Although the author can be said to make fun of the Roman people, he is not amused (C), nor is he frightened (D). The Roman people may be alarmist (E), but the author is not.

Question	Answer	Explanation
14	B	The people thought the earthquake was a sign that the world was declining, so they are indeed superstitious (B). The people affected by the earthquake came from Sicily, Dalmatia, Greece, and Egypt, so they were clearly not homogenous (A). There is no evidence that the people affected by the earthquake were "insightful" (D) or "reactionary" (C), nor is there any expression of regret (E).
15	A	The Romans were afraid because they saw the earthquake as a warning of even more destructive things to come (A). Saying that they were afraid because they commemorated the anniversary does not make sense (B). Because many Romans did not actually witness the flood, the spectator's view is not what scared them (C). Choice (D) is incorrect because their fear did not stem from remembering past earthquakes. The tide was destructive, but not necessarily fear-inspiring (E).
16	B	In the sentence "they considered these alarming strokes as the prelude only of still more dreadful calamities, and their fearful vanity was disposed to confound the symptoms of a declining empire and a sinking world," replace "declining" with the words "going downhill." Then, only (B), "worsening," makes sense.
17	E	The sentence "But the tide soon returned, with the weight of an immense and irresistible deluge, which was severely felt on the coasts of Sicily, of Dalmatia, of Greece, and of Egypt: large boats were transported, and lodged on the roofs of houses, or at the distance of two miles from the shore; the people, with their habitations, were swept away by the waters" makes it clear that the damage was primarily caused by a large flood (E). The city of Alexandria lost fifty thousand people; we are not told the total number of casualties (A). Homes were destroyed by the flood, not a tear in the earth (B). There is nothing that compares the severity of this earthquake with the earthquakes in Bithnyia and Palestine (C). There is no evidence that the tides were permanently affected (D).
18	C	All three sentences have verbs that are passive (as in "the book was read by Joe," as opposed to "Joe read the book" (C). There is no figurative language (i.e., a metaphor, simile) (A). The first sentence contains no adjectives (B). There is nothing oxymoronic, or internally contradictory, about the sentences (D). There are no analogies, nor is the setting a particularly pastoral or rural one (E).
19	B	The country life is "unvexed," meaning *lacking* cares and strife (B). None of the other choices mean "lacking."
20	C	The lines talk about the first couple, paired by God, who then are cursed and thrown out of Paradise: clearly Adam and Eve (C). The poet's wife is never mentioned (A). There is no evidence that the subject of the poem has a mistress, and the poet praises him for this (B). There is nothing to suggest that the poet is referencing Shakespeare (D), or a hypothetical pair of lovers (E).
21	E	The poet considers the country-dweller to be "blessed" and "unvexed" so the poet thinks that country life is excellent. Only "idyllic" fits this description (E).

Question	Answer	Explanation
22	E	The poet never mentions the effect of country life on health—"Enjoyed his youth, and now enjoys his age" does not refer to health but rather longevity (B). The poet does talk about a calm mind: "Like your own soul, serene, a pattern of your mind" (A). The poet does speak of friendship: "All who deserve his love, he makes his own; And, to be loved himself, needs only to be known" (C), and says that the country-dweller is "wise" (D).
23	D	The poet describes the subject as "uncumbered with a wife," so he finds a wife to be a burden and a source of strife (D). Marriage is not a necessity; the subject of the poem is not married (A), (B). The protracted lawsuit does not refer to marriage (C), nor is there evidence that the poet considers marriage to be a prison sentence (E).
24	A	The first six lines speak of a general "he," while the rest of the poem addresses the subject using "you" (A). There is no switch in tense (B), nor is there a general switch in attitude (C). There is no extended simile (D), and although God is mentioned in the last lines, there is no divine intervention (E).
25	D	The sentence reads, "Just, good, and wise, contending neighbors come, From your award to wait their final doom," so "their" refers to the contending neighbors (D). None of the others is the correct antecedent.
26	B	The "contending" (i.e., disagreeing) neighbors come for advice and to avoid law-suits, so the subject must play the role of a judge (B). There is no evidence that he is a farmer (A) or a religious leader (C). Similarly, nowhere in the poem does it suggest the subject is a writer (D) or scholar (E).
27	E	The first sentence has alliteration in "foes," "before," and "friendship." The second sentence has alliteration in "long litigious laws." The third contains alliteration in "penitence," "succeeds," and "short," in so (E) is the correct answer.
28	B	The poet is making the point that it's difficult to get along, and even Adam and Eve disagreed (B). The poet does not suggest that God punishes all couples, nor is equality the issue in the poem (A). "Matched" means "coupled," not necessarily "similar" (C). Choice (D) is too general a statement for the poem. Intelligence is not mentioned as a reason for being ostracized (E).
29	E	The poet uses all the listed words except "faith" as symbols of "heart" (E). The poet calls his heart "thou" in line 7 (A). "Reflector" is located on line 9 (B) and "record-er" on line 11 (C). The poet addresses his "Strong Heart" in line 1 (D).
30	B	The poet says his heart warned him when he began to think of evil thoughts, so "forming" is the best synonym (B). None of the others accurately fit the meaning.
31	D	The poet wants his heart to stay put and not break their bond. ("Hold yet a while, Strong Heart, Not part a lifelong yoke") (D). There is nothing in the passage that suggests an outside love (A). There is no mention of a failing heart ("Strong Heart") (B). The heart is clearly inside the poet, so it is not a separate being (C). He considers his heart a friend ("In thee is friendship"), not an enemy (E).

Question	Answer	Explanation
32	A	The poet speaks of rare smooth sailing and marching up and downhill for a long time, so (A) is the best answer. There is not a literal journey (and it is in the past) (B). There is no evidence of prison (C). Although the poet seems to find the water easier, there is no expression of regret (D). The poet speaks of a metaphoric journey, not a literal one (E).
33	A	All are mentioned except the theme of "love" (A). The poet calls his heart true (B). He mentions his "faith" (C). He says his heart warned him against "evil thoughts" or reminded him of his moral duties (D), and he speaks of a long time spent together (E).
34	A	In lines 8 and 11, an exclamation point and a question mark take the place of words (Statement 1). There is no consistent rhythm, and it does not reflect the theme (Statement 2). The form of the poem does not mirror its content (Statement 3).
35	B	The poet appears to be thanking his heart and coaxing it to stay, so "grateful" is the best answer (B). The poet is not "despairing" (A), nor is he "resigned" (C). There is no evidence of pride, and although there is a question mark, the poet does not employ a "questioning" tone (E).
36	C	The poet is comparing his heart to a recorder of thoughts, so it is a "metaphor" (C). There is no "alliteration" (A), "personification" (B), "paradox" (D), or "allegory" (E).
37	E	There is no evidence the men speak foreign languages ("various degrees of fluency" refers to their skill levels in the subjects, not foreign languages) (E). They are "youngish bachelors" and, therefore, unmarried (line 2) (A). Wilkinson did not "condescend" to speak with female teachers, and Coristine won't look at them (B). Wilkinson is a teacher, Coristine a lawyer (C). They both like books: "they were linked together by an ardent love of literature" (lines 23–24) (D).
38	C	Because Wilkinson is compared to Coristine, and "Coristine was a lawyer in full practice," then Wilkinson must have a position of responsibility in the school system (C). There is no mention of how well he was paid (A). There is also no discussion about how people feel about them (B). They are not eating, so they are not "sated" (D). Although they are well-dressed, this is not the focus of this line (E).
39	D	The young men are being contrasted to "respectable" church-members, so they must be unrespectable, or "dishonorable" (D). Although they may be "chauvinists," this sentence does not say that (A). There is no discussion of how talented they are (B). There is no evidence that they used to go to church (C), and because they do not go to church, they are not "pious" (E).
40	A	Wilkinson is described as "sedate" (line 14), so Coristine is in comparison the opposite, which is "excitable" (A). None of the other words conveys this meaning.

Question	Answer	Explanation
41	D	According to the men, women were "bringing the dignity of law and education to the dogs," so the men thought they were inferior (D). They had opportunities to meet women at work (A). There is no evidence in the passage that they felt threatened (B) or feared their jobs would be taken from them (C); although that may have been their subconscious fears, the passage never states this. They object to female teachers and clerks (E).
42	A	Coristine is a practicing lawyer, but his name is not part of the firm's name, so he is not valued by his firm (A). There is no discussion of his finances (B). There is nothing to suggest he works independently (C) or that he doesn't contribute sufficiently to the firm (D). He may indeed be at the beginning of his career, but this conclusion cannot be reached by the evidence in the passage (E).
43	B	The author makes fun of the characters as he paints them as snobs who consider themselves superior (B). The author is not offended (A), nor is the writing hesitant or overtly critical (C). The passage is not marked by extreme honesty (D) nor is it distant (E).
44	A	People were going to church as the young men went to their literary society, so "journeying to" is the best match (A). There is no evidence that they were in a hurry (B) or that they were late (E). And they were going, not coming (C), (D).
45	C	The line can be restated as "in trying to reclaim some virtue, the theater world's efforts have been wasted," so (C) is the best answer. None of the other words fits the sentence.
46	C	The line can be restated as "in trying to reclaim some virtue, the theater world's efforts have been wasted" so (C) is the best answer. The speaker does not think that actors are conceited (A), nor does the speaker claim that the theater is a home to those who don't believe in God (B). Although the passage speaks of labor, it is not the labor of acting (D). There is no evidence that the speaker is talking about the transformative power of theater (E).
47	B	A pen writing ("refrain"–ing) and having patience is an example of personification (B). None of the other phrases contains an example of personification.
48	C	Even if you don't know what triplets are, you can tell which answers are wrong. The poem has pairs of rhyming phrases and some phrases that come in rhyming sets of threes (C). There is a regular rhythm to the poem (A). There are triplets as well as couplets (B). Nothing is epic about the poem (D), and there are active as well as passive verbs (E).

Question	Answer	Explanation
49	B	From the lines "You care as little what the Poets teach, As you regard at Church what Parsons preach" (lines 4–5) it is clear that the author thinks people disregard what's said in church (B). It is not clear from the poem that the speaker thinks church is boring, only that he or she is aware that others do (A). There is no evidence that there is gossip in the church (C) or that the speaker considers the church a place for hypocrites (D). She does not compare church and state's superiority, but suggests only that people learn little from either (E).
50	B	The lines are sarcastic in that the speaker is mocking the people by saying that they learn as little from theater as they do from church (B). They are not an exaggeration (A). Although the tone is negative, it is not condemning (C). The speaker does not admire the theatergoers (D). In order for something to be parodical, it must be copying something else (E).
51	D	The poem states that people do everything in church and theater except conduct contests (D). They "ogle" (line 10) (A). They "snore" (line 8) (B). They "roar" (heckle the stage) (line 9) (C). They "get dully drunk" (line 9) (E).
52	B	The phrase describes snoring as a way of showing devotion, which is not possible (in fact, it's the opposite—if the churchgoers were devoted, they would be awake!), so "Hatefully praise" is the best match because praise is not a way to show hate (B). "Loudly read" is possible (A), as is "awkwardly leap" (C), so they cannot be the correct answers. Similarly, "forwardly slide" (D) and "piously stand" (E) are both possible—don't fall for the trap answer of picking "piously" because it's a synonym for "devoutly."
53	D	Each line of the poem has ten syllables. If "Y'" weren't elided with the following syllable, this line would have eleven syllables (uh-oh) so it's abbreviated to keep the meter even (D). Remember, you don't need any outside knowledge, so (A) can't be the answer. There is no evidence that the poet wanted to save copying time (B). In order to be alliteration, the similar sounds must be close together (C). A new subject is not being addressed (E).
54	C	The first paragraph introduces what people think about pirates. The second paragraph talks about how pirates feel guilty, so (C) is the best answer. Answer choice (A) is too general; the second paragraph doesn't really elaborate. There are no opposing viewpoints (B). The second paragraph does not justify the pirates' actions (D). Paragraph two's purpose is not to cite popular culture but rather to talk about pirates' feelings of guilt (E).